To Ali

"The altar must be
repaired, the truth must
be restored – but
the fire of God
must come down!"

(DML-J)

1 Kings 18

In His love

SENT BY JESUS

SENT BY JESUS

*

Some Aspects of
Christian Ministry
Today

'As the Father has sent me, so I send you.' (*John 20:21*)

*

DAVID BROUGHTON KNOX

THE BANNER OF TRUTH TRUST

THE BANNER OF TRUTH TRUST
3 Murrayfield Road, Edinburgh EH12 6EL
PO Box 621, Carlisle, Pennsylvania 17013, USA

*

© David Broughton Knox 1992
First published 1992
ISBN 0 85151 625 4

*

Typeset in 10½/12pt Linotron Plantin
At The Spartan Press Ltd, Lymington, Hants
Printed and bound in Great Britain by
Courier International Limited
East Kilbride, Scotland

TO

DENIS AND PAULINE RYAN

FAITHFUL IN FRIENDSHIP
FAITHFUL IN PRAYER
FAITHFUL SERVANTS OF THE WORD

Contents

Contents

Preface

The Christian ministry is currently experiencing many difficulties. Such a situation is not new but what is different today is the extent to which these difficulties arise from within the churches. In many denominations the qualifications traditionally regarded as necessary for the ministry have been set aside while in others the whole idea of men being set apart to teach the Word of God as a full-time vocation is called into question. One wrong tendency, namely, the tendency to regard the ministry of pastors as the *only* ministry in the church, has now been followed by a violent swing to another, and the work of public teaching and preaching is too often regarded as open to all who have the inclination.

Dr Broughton Knox has spent a lifetime in the training of preachers, missionaries and Christian workers and the present book is made up of some of his principal addresses on leadership in the churches. They present a cogent case for the need to go back to first principles. His primary concern is not with his own or with other denominations but to show that the way forward must be through renewed understanding of major biblical truths. Difficult though some of the questions are respecting the true role of an ordained ministry, Dr Knox believes that the Scriptures are well able to direct us. But we may need to think in fresh and sometimes radical ways.

This book is certainly no defence of the *status quo*. Nor

does it stop at the level of the intellectual. No mere re-organization or change of structures can secure men who are evidently sent by God. The real life of the churches depends upon their communion with heaven and the first qualification of men who will serve the cause of Christ is that they should be men of prayer who know God in his word.

We are particularly indebted to the Rev. Denis Ryan of Sydney for his aid in the assembling of this material. It now goes to press with the publishers' conviction that it possesses an importance far beyond its size.

THE PUBLISHERS, January 1992

1
The Nature of the Christian Ministry

Times are changing, society is changing, changes are going on in church life and in the form of the Christian ministry. What are the features of the ministry which must not be allowed to change? We must first ask, 'What is the ministry?' How do we define it? It may, perhaps, be described as a full-time life occupation serving the Christian congregation. But is such full-time service justified and, if so, what form should it take?

There are lots of occupations in which men and women spend their lives and which are forms of service to the Christian congregation. For example, in an old-fashioned church, the verger has a full-time occupation serving the congregation; and people who work in central church offices, whether as administrators or typists, may be said to be giving their life to serving Christian congregations. But none of those who are engaged in these occupations would say that they are essential biblical ministries, useful though they are in our present circumstances. So the question must be faced, 'Is there an essential full-time Christian ministry which has its roots in the New Testament?'

From one point of view every Christian has a ministry. God gives gifts to each of us and we serve him as we use these gifts for other people's benefit. This is our ministry and it is a Christian ministry, so that, if all ministries are similar, then none can be full-time, none can require the special support of the congregation.

There are three passages in the New Testament which speak of different ministries in the church – Romans 12, 1 Corinthians 12 and Ephesians 4 – and it is plain that not all of these ministries are full-time ministries to which men or women might devote their whole lifetime. For example, prophecy. We read of Agabus and the four daughters of Philip the evangelist who prophesied; but prophecy is intermittent and is not a full-time occupation. It does not, for example, require preparation but is uttered as the Spirit moves the Christian. Other gifts mentioned in these passages, such as speaking in tongues or interpretation of tongues, would not be full-time occupations, nor would the gifts of healing or the working of miracles.

On the other hand, there are examples of full-time ministries in the New Testament. Pre-eminent is the ministry of Jesus who, in the period of time covered by the Gospels, gave himself exclusively to his ministry, which was that of teaching and proclaiming the imminence of God's rule. Teaching was the most conspicuous aspect of Jesus' ministry, for it was by the title of 'teacher' that he was known to the general public. This is disguised in our old-fashioned English by the word 'master', but 'teacher' is a more accurate translation. A typical Gospel statement describing Jesus' activity during the three years he travelled around Galilee and Judea is in Matthew 9:35:

Jesus went about all the cities and villages, teaching in their synagogues, and preaching the gospel of the kingdom, and healing all manner of sickness.

Christ taught the character of God's rule and he used numerous parables to illustrate various aspects of the rule, or kingdom, of God.

Signs of God's kingdom accompanied his preaching – signs of healing and of casting out demons – and these signs were in accordance with what the Old Testament foretold, so that all who knew their Old Testament Scriptures would have recognized that Jesus was the Messiah. In New Testament times, however, the signs of the presence of God's kingdom are no longer the Old Testament outward signs so much as the interior signs of the change of heart. Paul states that the kingdom of God is *righteousness*, that is, a restored relationship to God; *peace*, that is, a restored relationship to one another; and *joy in the Holy Spirit*, a restored relationship of our own interior spirit.

Another example of full-time ministry in the New Testament is that of Paul himself. His was an itinerant apostleship, which was, by its very character and of necessity, a full-time occupation, for he was the apostle to the Gentiles and so travelled throughout the Mediterranean world. He spent three years in the important city of Ephesus. Here we read that he taught daily in a public lecture room (*Acts 19:9*), and we know that he added to this a teaching ministry in the homes of his hearers. Paul himself describes the content of his ministry as giving to Christians a world view in which God and the Lord Jesus Christ were the centre; that is, he taught, as he put it, 'the whole counsel of God, holding back nothing that was profitable for you to know' (*Acts 20:20,27*). He also described his ministry as a proclamation of the kingdom of God, because teaching the whole counsel of God and proclaiming the kingdom of God are two aspects of the one activity. Christ was, of course, the centre of his preaching, or proclamation, and he described his activity in another way when he called it 'preaching the good news of the grace of God' or, again, when he described his work at Ephesus as a calling for 'repentance towards God and faith towards our Lord Jesus Christ'.

We see, then, from Acts 19 and 20, how Paul filled up his time at Ephesus. It was a full-time ministry, teaching about God's activity in Jesus. This teaching was, of course, pastorally centred, in the sense that it was directed to people's needs so as to evoke a response; and so the teaching would not be dry or arid but would contain both exhortation and admonition. He himself said that, for three years at Ephesus, he admonished the Christians 'night and day with tears' (*Acts 20:31*).

Consideration of the character of the Christian religion shows that there will always be a place for full-time ministry of the Word of God. The Christian religion is a religion of faith in Christ the Lord. Faith is distinguished from superstition by being based on the truth, and distinguished from rashness by being based on the knowledge of the truth. All this depends on true *teaching*, for we are not born with a knowledge of the truth. Moreover, Christianity is a religion of personal relationship, that is, of fellowship. Fellowship comes only through hearing and responding to a word spoken. So it is plain that a ministry which conveys and makes clear the truth about God and conveys God's Word to the mind, and so to the conscience of the hearer is an essential characteristic of Christianity. If this ministry dies out, then Christianity dies out.

The same conclusion may be arrived at from a slightly different approach. Jesus Christ is Lord but he can exercise no lordship, nor can obedience be the response of the Christian, unless the mind of Christ is known and known relevantly to the circumstances of the Christian. This, again, requires a teaching ministry which understands the mind of Christ and how it applies to modern circumstances, and which accompanies this teaching with exhortation and admonition directed to the conscience of the hearer. A ministry of Christian teaching and preaching is a lifetime occupation, because teaching cannot be discharged without preparation, and preparation requires time. For the Christian teacher to give himself to preparation, to the study of the Word of God and its relevance, was never more needed than in the present generation. New questions keep on looming

[4]

up, such as the rightness of nuclear war, abortion, such theories as evolution and so on. If the Christian teacher is to guide the minds of the Christian congregation aright, he must give himself to a good deal of reading and reflection. The unprepared teacher and preacher is like the blind guide.

* * *

There are many ways in which a Christian may spend his life and earn his living to God's glory and to the benefit of his fellow men. How are we to distinguish those excellent and Christian lifetime occupations from the essential Christian ministry?

Perhaps the test is whether a person has the opportunity in them of proclaiming the kingdom of God and of teaching the whole counsel of God by instruction, exhortation and admonition. It is true that every Christian has opportunity, from time to time, of doing these things. Yet some are called by God to give the whole of their time to these things; and if they have no independent means, other Christians make this possible by supporting them. Those who occupy most of their time in this way may be designated as Christian ministers.

The question is whether such excellent occupations as school teaching, social counselling, hospital or migrant chaplaincies, church administration, theological teaching and so on ought to be regarded as forms of the Christian ministry. On the definition above, the test to be applied is: What opportunity do they give for proclamation and teaching the Christian faith? Even if these activities are not included in the Christian ministry, they may be regarded as directly assisting that ministry. A verger who keeps a church clean would certainly be regarded as assisting the ministry. Not all of them, however, could be designated as directly assisting the Christian ministry; some ought to be regarded as humanitarian activities, alongside such occupations as the medical profession, the nursing profession or occupational therapy.

It is possible to be a selfish doctor and to be in medicine for what you can make out of it, but it still remains true that medicine is a direct service to other people. The same is true of social counselling. Doubtless, Christians, whether ordained or lay, who enter such professions as social counselling or school teaching, are not motivated by selfish reasons, though there is always a temptation to fall into selfishness. Even the minister in the parish is not exempt from such temptation, any more than is any other Christian. But the fact that a man carries out his work unselfishly in a profession of immediate help to people does not, in itself, make it the Christian ministry. Nor does it become the Christian ministry simply because it is controlled by a church body such as a synod. Nor is it the Christian ministry because the man who is performing it has been ordained. The test that is suggested is whether or not it gives full opportunity for preaching and teaching, with necessary time for prayer and preparation, which are essential for such preaching and teaching.

*　　*　　*

The Christian church, which is a heavenly concept and which, translated into factual terms, means 'fellowship with God and with one another through the blood of Christ', expresses itself in the here and now in our fellowship with each other in the name of Christ in local gatherings of which Christ says he is in the midst.

Because of human nature and the structure of human life, these local fellowships, which are the way that the concept of the church exists on earth, form patterns and structures and recognized ministries both within them and linking them. These structures which the church – that is, the heavenly fellowship – of necessity creates in a world of space and time are visible in the sense that other people, who are not Christians, can recognize the structures quite easily. They therefore become institutions in society, taking their place with all the other institutions that go to form a society or community.

Institutions are the framework of society and healthy Christian institutions make a healthy Christian society. The members and ministers of the church must recognize that, though they are primarily members of a heavenly entity, they are also members of a human society which is not fully Christ-centred and that their church with its institutions (including its ministry) and its denominational structures are important elements in the social structures of the society of which they themselves are members. This implies that the Christian minister has not only a spiritual role but also an institutional and social role and that he cannot ignore this latter concomitant of his ministry without injuring the human society and community of which he is a member and, consequently, to which he has a duty.

On the other hand, the minister must remember that his primary work – that is, the primary way of spending his time – is that of prayer and ministry of the Word, so that his institutional capacity in society must not be allowed to erode his time and energy so that he cannot give himself to the ministry of the Word and prayer. For if he fails in this prior function of being a Christian minister, his institutional function will cease to be a beneficial element in the structures of society, and the unique contribution of the Christian structures to the structures of our society will be lost.

One further point should be added. It is possible for a Christian minister to mistake what his function should be as a Christian minister. A good example of this is provided by a book I once read about a church in a typical English town. The author's description of the parish rang very true. He wrote of a vicar and his wife who were discouraged that,

[7]

after several years of work, they had not achieved their objective. This objective, we are told, was also regarded as a proper one for the ministry, both by the bishop and a missioner and his team. It is plainly regarded as a proper objective by the writer of the book, for he does not suggest an alternative. His only interest seemed to be in finding a better method of achieving the commonly agreed objective, and this, he believed, lay in better methods of communication. But the main objective is wrong and, therefore, not achieved; hence the sense of frustration felt by the writer of the book, as well as by the innumerable vicars and their wives whom he truly described.

The agreed and assumed objective appeared to be to increase church attendance from between 30 and 50 to, say, 500. This would be regarded as success because it would fill the church building to overflowing. But why 500 rather than 50 should be regarded as the objective when there are probably 10,000 people in the parish is not explained. Moreover, simply improving methods of communication will not lift the 50 to 500, except in unusual circumstances. The real objective ought not to be to persuade more people to participate in the institutionalized liturgy and congregational activities but rather to create a true fellowship in Christ amongst those who live in the area so that, into this fellowship, others may be converted by the public and private proclamation of the gospel. Fellowship can exist only in the area of truth, that is, reality, and there is something unreal in any primary concern to bring people to the church to participate in a prearranged institutional activity, as though the congregation was a consequent to the arranging of the church service, instead of the service and liturgy being consequent to the congregation's presence.

There is a profound difference between coming to church in order to be together, that is to express the heavenly fellowship in praying, praising and listening to God's Word (for these then become real fellowship activities which all participate in, even if they are only sitting silently and listening with mental response) – between this and coming to an activity which is conceived of as existing independently of the coming together.

So long as we think of our church activity in this latter way, we will not be able to avoid an air of unreality. There will be an absence of fellowship and even the finest communication and exhortation will not persuade people to participate in such an activity. Strictly speaking, it is difficult to see any reason why they should, and people will be aware of this, even if they cannot articulate the reason for it.

*   *   *

Returning, then, to the question with which we began this chapter, we may say that while all Christians have ministries, there are important reasons why servants of the Word are designated as ministers of God. They have been sent by God in response to the prayers of his people (*Matt. 9:38*). They are his messengers (literally, his angels) to bring his Word to his people, to the sheep whom the Father has given to Jesus. Not everyone is so sent by God for such ministry. When a man is called by God to this work, he is called to something to which he must devote his life. His ministry is an essential ministry in the purposes of God for the maintenance of faith and obedience and the calling of people into fellowship with God. It will not be without tears, as Paul experienced at Ephesus, nor without dangers. Christ's teaching led to his crucifixion. His ministers must also teach and bear the trials that follow. They – along with all Christians – may triumph in Christ's strength and reign with him now and eternally (*Eph. 2:6; 2 Tim. 2:12*). They are sharers in Christ's sufferings for the same purpose that he suffered, namely the blessing of the sheep that the Father has given him (*Col. 1:24; 2 Cor. 1:5, 6*). To those sent by God to this ministry there is no more worthwhile way of spending their lives.

2
The Theology of Ordination

In understanding the nature of ordination, it is first necessary to understand the nature of the church. The church forms itself spontaneously. The Lord Jesus Christ sends his messengers to preach the good news of God. Those who believe this news and call on the name of the Lord are accepted by God and adopted as his sons and daughters. This is sealed by God's giving himself to them through the Spirit indwelling their hearts and teaching them to relate to God as their heavenly Father (*Gal. 4:6*). In this way, in Christ, they have access to the Father's presence, and stand as it were in his royal court, in fellowship with him and with their brethren in Christ. Together they form a great assembly or congregation or church in the heavenlies. Naturally, they give expression to this heavenly fellowship, which goes on continuously, by forming earthly fellowships in the neighbourhood in which they live, as opportunity allows. Thus from the beginning, Christian congregations or churches formed spontaneously. Those who believed the gospel, drawn by God's Holy Spirit indwelling each, sought fellowship with one another in their common faith and hope and gave expression to the love for one another which the Spirit taught them.

In these congregations, God set leaders. First in time and logic were apostles who had been commissioned by Christ himself. They were the witnesses to the great facts of the gospel, who brought this news to the localities where these

Christian believers lived. Then there were prophets who filled out the Christian revelation by the direct inspiration of the Holy Spirit. Thirdly, there were teachers who expounded the knowledge of this revelation and applied it to the life situation of the members of the congregation (*1 Cor. 12*). In Ephesians 4, Paul adds a fourth group, evangelists. They were proclaimers of the news, though not themselves being of the apostolic band. Timothy was an evangelist.

In Ephesians 4, Paul described teachers as 'pastors and teachers'. The words are closely linked in the Greek, for pastoring in spiritual things is teaching the Word of God by applying it (in general and in particular) to the situation of the hearer; and it is nothing more. In 1 Corinthians 12 Paul adds, after teachers, a list of spiritual activities which may be found in the church or congregation. In Ephesians the list is confined to ministers of the Word. It is proclaimers of his life-giving Word that the ascended Christ gives as his gift to mankind (*Eph. 4:8, 11*).

Each congregation is complete, for Christ is present and through his Spirit he makes the congregation sufficient for supplying the needs of its members. It is the church of God. Each congregation could be described as independent of other congregations, if the word 'independent' were a suitable one to describe Christian relationships. But since we all stand together in the heavenly congregation, joining in the eternal presence of the seven Spirits of God, it is not appropriate to describe our relationship to our fellow Christians as one of 'independence'. By the same token, it is not appropriate to describe the relationship of congregation to congregation as one of independence. Nevertheless, although congregations have love and concern for one another, no-one *outside* the congregation can be a God-given leader *in* the congregation, and certainly should not be a director of the congregation in any of its spiritual activities. However, exhortation and encouragement of one another is the duty of all Christians, both when they are within the congregation and when they are not.

In the ordination of those who minister the Word of God in the congregation, the first prerequisite is that God should send the minister, for God sends his prophets and teachers and will never fail to do so. He 'rises up early and sends them' to his congregation. (This 'sending' does not imply geographical movement any more than 'commissioning' does.) This sending of God will largely show itself through the natural gifts with which he endows his servants, such as gifts of intelligence, knowledge and rational ability. In the Christian congregation (which comes into being because of a common love for Christ and of one another, and a common hope and expectation of his return) those who possess these gifts of spiritual leadership will certainly be prompted by the Spirit to use them in the spiritual strengthening and help for the members of the congregation as they perceive their fellow Christians' needs. That is, spiritual leadership will find expression and come to the surface naturally in Christ's congregation which has formed itself spontaneously and naturally as a result of believing the gospel. We see this process at work in 1 Corinthians 16, where the household of Stephanas have appointed themselves to minister to their fellow Christians, and Paul directs the Corinthian Christians to recognize this and to subject themselves to such ministers and to everyone who joins in the work and labours in it. It was not only the household of Stephanas but also Fortunatus and Achaicus who were encouraging the spirits of the Corinthians. Paul tells the church that they are to take knowledge of such people. It is plain that in the church at Corinth there was not yet any formally ordained minister, although the church had been formed for some two years at least. It was Paul's practice to allow a time to elapse after the first preaching of the gospel and the first turning of converts to Christ, before the formalizing of the ministry in that congregation. Thus it is only on his return visit to the churches of Southern Asia Minor that he appointed elders in each church (*Acts 14*). Doubtless this was to allow a time-lag so that it would become obvious who it was that God was sending as ministers of his Word in each church. The same time-lag is plain in Paul's ministry in Crete. He left the island having established churches in every town, but not having formalized the appointment of any ministers; this was still 'wanting' (*Titus 1:5*). 1 Corinthians shows how the ministry was formed to the point of full recognition. Firstly, there was the Spirit of God in the hearts of those to whom he had given gifts and opportunities to minister to their fellow members, who prompted them to minister as they saw the need. Then there was the duty, which Paul underlined, of the members of the congregation to recognize these gifts and this ministry which God had given them and set in their congregation. They were to recognize (*epiginōskō*) these ministers and submit themselves to their ministry.

Thus ordination is primarily the public recognition by the congregation of those whom God has sent as ministers of his Word in that congregation (i.e. church) of God. But ordination has another closely related element. It must be remembered that it is the duty of the ministers in the congregation to care for the spiritual welfare of that congregation and one of the primary areas of care is the continuance of the ministry of God's Word within the congregation. Thus Paul reminded Timothy that it fell within his ministerial duty to see that the ministry of God's Word was effectively continued. Just as he had received the truth from Paul and his fellows, he was to hand it on to faithful men who would be able to teach others also (*2 Tim. 2:2*) – four generations of apostolic succession in the apostolic word. And Paul's care for the churches in Crete included his care for ensuring that they had a recognized Christian ministry.

[14]

It may therefore be said that by ordination there is a twofold recognition of the minister whom God has set in the congregation. Firstly, it is the public recognition by the congregation itself. Its members have a duty to recognize those who have been moved by the Spirit of God to use their gifts and opportunities in this essential way of ministry. Secondly, it is also the recognition by the present ministers of new ministers who are being sent by God to share the ministry with them and, in due course, take their place.

In valid ordination, three elements are necessary:

1) The conviction in the heart of the ordinand that God has sent him to this ministry. If the Holy Spirit does not give him this conviction, it is highly unlikely that he is sending him at this time to this work.

2) Recognition by those in a position best to recognize it, of the reality of the ministry of those whom God sends to the church as his messengers.

3) Recognition by the Spirit-filled obedient Christian congregation of the ministers whom God is sending them, and whom they are to honour for their work's sake and to whom they are to submit within their ministry (*Heb. 13:17*).

Ordination is recognition of God-given ministry by the congregation led by its spiritual leaders. It is not, of course, a sacrament, for it is not in itself a means of grace; that is, it is not in itself designed to lead to a deeper relationship with Christ.

Ordination is a Christian duty, not on the part of the ordinand, but on the part of those who receive the ministry. The Christian congregation is obligated to recognize and submit, within the sphere of their ministry, to those whom God sends as his messengers. Also, the members of the congregation should be helped in this by formal recognition through ordination at the hands of their present ministers, who should complement and lead in this way the spiritual discernment of the congregation. Those ordained are ordained for the ministry in the church of God, that is to say, in the congregation. If God sends his messenger to one congregation, and if circumstances mean that this person moves to another congregation, it may be assumed that God is now sending him to that congregation. But this does not obviate the duty of the congregation, perhaps through its representatives, of recognizing and confirming that God has sent this messenger to them. Ordination and induction are identical concepts, except that the word ordination is reserved for the first recognition by the church that God is sending his servant to be his messenger to his people. The place of the congregation in ordination is primary but it is not unilateral. A Christian congregation is not independent, but is in fellowship with other congregations amongst whom Christ is also present as their Lord. Therefore, in recognizing a messenger from God, a congregation should act in fellowship with other congregations.

Ordination brings these benefits, namely, that it explicates to the congregation their recognition of God's minister to them and so makes it easier for them to know to whom they should submit, as Paul enjoins the Corinthians to do. It also assists the minister himself by making explicit to him that he is God's messenger and therefore is not to neglect the ministry, but rather to bestir himself in exercising this gift entrusted to him as designated by the Spirit and accompanied with the laying on of the hands of his fellow ministers in the church (*1 Tim. 4:14*).

*   *   *

A lot of Christians these days speak as though all gifts for ministry in the body of Christ are of equal importance. But this is not so. Some are crucial, some more peripheral. Paul recognized a hierarchy in gifts and urged his readers to seek 'the greater gifts' (*1 Cor. 12:31; cf. 14:1*).

The greatest privilege that God gives to any of his children in this life is to be in the apostolic succession. It is not a succession of tactile ordination through the laying on of hands, as it was distorted in the centuries after the apostles, but a succession of receiving and teaching the apostolic message on which our faith and hope and eternal life are based. Timothy was in this apostolic succession, as are all true ministers of the Word of life today. Paul told Timothy 'the things which thou hast heard from me among many witnesses, the same commit thou to faithful men, who shall be able to teach others also' (*2 Tim. 2:2; cf. 2 Tim. 1:13*).

The apostolic succession is to receive and teach to others the unchanging eternal news of God. This is the vital ministry in the body of Christ. The exercise of every other gift in ministry depends on this. If this ministry of the Word of God is defective, every other ministry, for example, exhortation, encouragement and admonition, will be defective and indeed erroneous.

3
The Mission of the Church and the Purpose of the Ministry

The most explicit passage in the New Testament describing the mission of the church is in Ephesians where Paul states that his preaching to the Gentiles the gospel of the unsearchable riches of Christ is with the ultimate object of making clear to the heavenly beings the extraordinary and many-sided wisdom of God (*Eph. 3:8, 10; cf. Rev. 14:1–3*). That is to say, the mission of the church is to manifest and make plain the character of God to the denizens of heaven and this is in accordance with the New Testament concept that the church is essentially a heavenly entity. It is an assembly of the redeemed gathered round God in heaven (*Heb. 12:22, 23*). As Christ adds to this assembly of saints more and more converts from every tribe, nation and language, God's gracious character and extraordinary wisdom are made evident. He is seen to be a God who justifies the ungodly, yet not in the corrupt way of a venal human judge, but in a way through which he remains absolutely and completely just and righteous.

The world does not recognize the nobility of the work of God in transforming sinners into Christlike persons, nor his power in overthrowing the strongholds of Satan. This work of God proceeds unnoticed by the secular historian. But the angels of heaven see it and glorify God for it. Indeed, the Scriptures suggest that they are keenly interested in the unfolding of God's plan and purposes of salvation (*1 Pet. 1:12; Dan. 8:13*). There is joy in heaven when a rebellious sinner, released from the power of darkness, joins the heavenly court on his conversion (*Lk. 15:7; Eph. 2:18; Col. 1:13; Heb. 10:19; 12:22*). The gathering of the nations into the heavenly church through the gospel redounds to God's glory in the heavenlies. 'The obedience of the Gentiles' brought about through the gospel and the working of the Holy Spirit (*Rom. 15:18*) was and is a most remarkable thing.

That Christians are, during their earthly life, members of the heavenly city of God is a truth reiterated in several places in the New Testament. Thus in Galatians 4:26 the heavenly Jerusalem (where God in reality dwells) is said to be our true mother city. It was of her that the prophet spoke, as inhabited by innumerable children, in contrast with the earthly Jerusalem whose children were carried away into captivity. Paul reverts to the heavenly citizenship of Christians in Philippians 3:20, reminding his readers that 'our citizenship is in heaven'. The fact that Christians have been given access to God's throne and indeed that they stand in his presence is a truth which is expressed frequently in the New Testament. This is another way of asserting that Christians, God's little ones, are in heaven even while living on earth. Their spirits are always beholding the face of their Father in heaven. Their heavenly existence is their real existence and the heavenly assembly of which they are part is the real assembly, *ecclēsia* or church, of which the local assemblies are the earthly and transitory counterparts or expressions.

These local assemblies have no function except to be true expressions of the heavenly church. Their members should express those characteristics and engage in those actions which make the heavenly church glorious and which redound to God's praise. The principle for behaviour in church is the divine principle of service. This involves gathering in each other's company to build each other up in the holy faith. Christians in church are to encourage one another in attitudes and actions of love and good works, strengthening one another in the hope of the coming of the Lord (*Heb. 10:25*). They are to engage together in prayer and praise and thanksgiving to God (*Col. 3:16; Eph. 5:19, 20; 1 Cor. 14*), teaching one another, exhorting one another and admonishing one another.

The church, that is, the heavenly church, is the assembly whose members have been redeemed and transformed. They are the people of faith, each one of whom is to glorify God by the way he lives his life. In this way the church sets forth the excellences of God whose mercy has created a people from those who were not his people (*1 Pet. 2:9, 10*). Though Peter expresses in this passage a vivid concept of the unity of Christians – a people, a race, a nation – the duties he enjoins by which God's excellences will be demonstrated are individual. He has no concept that Christians should combine to achieve such objects as social justice. The members of the local congregation are to live their Christian lives each in their own circumstances. These will redound to God's glory. But though Peter in this passage makes clear that the life of the Christian is essentially heaven-oriented, and that it sets forth God's excellences, he does not especially say, as does Paul, that the good life of the Christian redounds to God's glory in the heavenlies. Nevertheless, the unseen life glorifies God. The 'meek and quiet spirit' of the 'hidden person of the heart' is in the sight of God of great worth (*1 Pet. 3:4*).

A great deal of Christian living is unobserved or if observed, misunderstood and not valued by the non-Christian, who is blind to the things of the Spirit. But such lives are not unobserved in the heavenlies. Jesus said that every Christian conversion brings joy in the presence of God, and every Christian action doubtless does the same.

If the church's mission is centred on this earth, it must be considered as much a failure as a success. Promising ministers, such as were many of the Reformers, and later many pioneer missionaries, have been cut off by martyrdom. Flourishing Christian communities, such as the early African churches or the Nestorian churches of the East, vanished through ruthless persecution. But their witness, unnoticed or scorned on earth and without apparent effect, was noticed in heaven, where God is ceaselessly praised for his wonderful works in gathering out a people from rebellious humanity and transforming them into the image of Christ, the image of God. (*Rev. 7:9–12*, especially *v. 11*).

The minister is God's fellow-worker in bringing to fruition this gracious purpose of God. The apostle Paul was overwhelmed with the grace given to him, the less than the least of all Christians, that he might be the minister of God to preach to the nations the unsearchable riches of Christ, with the ultimate purpose that the heavenly beings might know the marvellous, many-sided depths of the wisdom of God who created all things (*Eph. 3:7–13*).

Ministers share this ministry with Paul. Let it ever be remembered that the ultimate end of this ministry is heavenly, not earthly.

4
The Ministry and Teaching

The Christian minister's task is to make known the news that God's judgment is very close and that God will judge every one of us without exception by his standard of absolute righteousness, absolute justice, absolute goodness and absolute obedience. Every action will be judged, even the idle word. At that judgment, God's anger will be expressed towards many in their eternal and absolute separation from his presence. They will go into the outer darkness, from which all good influences are excluded. They will be shut up in a den of thieves where everyone is preying on some other, everyone assaulting some other, everyone doing some other down, everyone hating some other. There will be no friendship, no kindness, no love, and no presence of God at all.

This is the plain teaching of Scripture, the plain and repeated teaching of Jesus, and plain common sense. It is inevitable, and unavoidable through our own efforts, because none of us can blot out the past. We have already placed ourselves fairly and squarely and unavoidably under God's condemnation at the judgment day, whether this is at death or at the end of the world, both of which are very near to each of us.

To put it another way, and in the biblical phraseology to which we have become so accustomed, the Christian minister is to preach that the kingdom of heaven is at hand. This is what John the Baptist preached; this is what Jesus preached; this is what the apostles preached, and this is what Jesus has sent us to preach, 'As the Father hath sent me, even so send I you', he said (*John 20:21*). God's kingdom is God's rule as King and it is the first duty of the King to keep law and order, to praise those who do well and to punish those who do wrong. As we all know, one breach of the law, one crime, deserves punishment, and if there is any justice in our society, it receives it. So too with God. He is the righteous King of his universe and his Word makes clear that he will not overlook evil. God is the righteous judge of all the earth. He will reward with eternal life those who persevere in doing right all the time, in every circumstance, doing right by God and by their neighbour, and he will judge and condemn all who do wrong, any wrong.

The Old Testament and the New Testament state clearly: Cursed by God is everyone who does not continue all his life doing everything that is right (*Deut. 27:26; Gal. 3:10*). None of us is able to attain that standard, which is the standard of heaven. Only one of all who have ever lived on this earth's surface has persevered all through life in doing the right thing by his neighbour and by God. That one is Jesus of Nazareth. He has been crowned with the reward and it is only through him that any of us can escape the just judgment of our turning aside from what we know to be right. We may not turn aside all the time, we may not reach the utmost depths of sin. But heaven requires perfection, so if we are to reach that happy place, and to avoid the doom that is the alternative, it will only be through our relationship with Jesus, who did God's will perfectly in perfect love, perfect faith and perfect obedience in every circumstance that came his way.

So the Christian minister not only preaches that the kingdom of heaven is at hand, but he also preaches that all who call upon the name of Jesus will be saved. Their sins will be forgiven and blotted out so completely that God will no longer see them. They will be received, as Jesus is, into God's presence the moment they turn to God in the name of Jesus.

That is news to the great majority of the earth's population at the present moment. Everybody knows that guilt deserves punishment and that they are, in many respects, guilty of many things; but few know of the marvellous salvation which the love of God has provided in sending his Son to be the Saviour of the world.

The Christian pastor is not only to proclaim the news of judgment and salvation, the news that Jesus is the judge (*Acts 10:42*) and also the rescuer from the wrath, or anger, of God which will soon overtake us. He has an equally important ministry committed to him, namely, to teach those who respond to this news and turn to God. In his last words to his disciples, Jesus commanded them to make the nations learners and to bring them into the knowledge of the full character of the triune God by teaching them everything that he had commanded them (*Matt. 28:20*). Proclamation of the news and the teaching of those who respond are not two things but one. If the teaching is true, there will always be an opportunity for expounding the gospel to those who are listening to the exposition of Scripture with its teaching content. When a hearer responds to the gospel and puts his faith in Christ, God works in his heart so that from now on he wants to learn about God, instead of trying to avoid him and blot him out of his mind. He is anxious to be taught and he needs teaching. He needs to know the whole counsel of God if he is going to grow and be useful as a Christian. It is the minister's task to teach those who come anxious to learn. It is not his job to amuse them or entertain them so that they come back next time. He is to teach those who want to know about God, and that means he must expound God's Word, for there only is where the knowledge of God is to be found.

The enormous need of teaching in the Christian congregation by its minister has been borne in on me very dramatically in recent years by the fact that I have become a grandfather and my grandchildren are now growing up at school. These are formative years for them. Their parents are diligently teaching them at home, but when they take them to church on Sunday, there is nothing worth listening to. The Bible is no longer read in the way it used to be – a chapter from the Old Testament and a chapter from the New at each service. It is no longer expounded carefully and applied to common life. Youth services do little more, it would seem, than sing choruses which are often sentimental and centred on oneself. It is desperately hard to find any church where God's Word is consistently and fully taught. Too often, ministers are well-meaning but they do not know what their job is. They do not know that without clear, consistent teaching the eager young mind is not able to develop, so that an adult life lived for the next forty years in modern secular society can retain its knowledge and relationship with God. Without regular teaching there can be no building up of such faith as leads to faithful obedience and witness in daily life. The result of this widespread lack of knowledge, through lack of teaching, means that all sorts of sects are springing up, and within the churches all sorts of alternative ways of conducting Christian fellowship meetings are being adopted. Some of them are very colourful, but they remind one of the fungus that grows on a rotting tree – colourful and attractive, but mostly poisonous to the spiritual life.

Why is it that Christian ministers seem to have so poor an understanding of the ministry to which they are committed? It can only be that they themselves have not been taught and so are unable to teach others. They have not been taught what their ministry is, so they are not discharging it, though they think that they are. Since they get such discouraging results, they may abandon it or turn to counselling and other helping ministries which appear to be so rewarding. Spiritual ministry may not be rewarding in this life, but it is of eternal permanence.

The teaching of children should begin in their homes by their parents, who ought to make it the top priority in their children's welfare. But it should be supported by the teaching ministry of the parish minister. There is no need for him to separate the children out from the congregation to be taught by adolescents in Sunday School. He is the teacher of the congregation, which includes children, and he must discharge that duty faithfully so that all present may learn. Parents must be supported by the Sunday ministry in bringing up their children in the fear and nurture of the Lord. Not only should the children be taught by the sermon, but the parents should be taught so that they can effectively teach their children at home during the week. Unless we understand clearly the whole counsel of God, we will not be able to maintain a faithful ministry so that we ourselves can teach others, as we have the opportunity.

All this depends on the minister of the congregation. He is occupying that place, and it might well be the only congregation with which it is convenient for the family to meet. If the minister is not teaching the whole counsel of God, then he will be held responsible for failing to nurture God's sheep. For they have no other shepherd available to them. This is my problem with my grandchildren. Where can they go? Where will their parents' efforts at home be supported by the minister of a Christian congregation?

A test for a minister to apply to his own ministry is this: are the parents in the congregation able to teach their children the whole counsel of God and to answer their questions, especially teenage questions, and are they doing it? If they are not able to, the minister's teaching is at fault. If they are not doing it, his exhortation is at fault.

Unless Christians know the whole counsel of God, that is to say, unless they have a world view that is centred on God and his work in Christ, centred on eternal things, on judgment and salvation, unless they have a true basis of heavenly values by which they are to live their lives and direct their efforts, they will not be able to maintain their Christian witness in the world or their own relationship with God. They need to be taught all their lives, in order that they might live close to their Lord and Saviour. One is not born with a Christian world view. We must be taught by those who have been Christians before us. Sadly, the teaching that is being given at present in Christendom is almost nil, and this fact is very clearly brought home when we search for a congregation near at hand where our family will receive the instruction which we need for Christian living, and daily Christian hope and faith and joy and endurance.

Many, very many preachers think that they are teaching when all that they are doing is exhorting their congregations on the basis of elementary knowledge previously gained, or else they impart their theological system with their exhortations, as they have done in their previous sermons. In neither case is the congregation stimulated to grow in the knowledge of God and it diminishes in number. For a congregation to grow in knowledge the preacher must expound what is in the text or the passage, controlling his exhortation by the context. There will always be something fresh that God is saying in the passage and if this is brought out clearly, the listeners will grow in their knowledge of what God is saying to them, and will rejoice as they grow.

But for the preacher's part, he must set aside time for study, for preparation and for prayer.

5
Prepare and Preach Properly, or Perish

On visits to different churches a twofold phenomenon has impressed itself on my mind. The first is the emptiness of some of the sermons I have heard. They have been well constructed, and delivered with a good deal of eloquence and ability, but they have had no content; they have been empty. Though the structure was good, and the vocabulary and delivery showed that the preachers were experienced, they were saying nothing of any significance. I am not surprised that no-one comes to hear them.

The reason for this emptiness is that there has not been proper preparation, because the ministers are so busy in other excellent things that they do not have the time for preparation. They learn to deliver sermons with a minimum amount of preparation but with a lot of experience and skill in delivery. But however well polished, an empty sermon will result in empty churches. The sermon that is full of teaching about God cannot be delivered without thorough preparation. First, there is required the long-term preparation of constant reading and thinking about God and the world, and our relationship with God, and his purposes. Secondly, there is required the intense short-term preparation that needs to go into each sermon.

But these days ministers are so busy building up their congregations by every method other than the preparation of their addresses that they have no time to prepare properly.

Twice this last week I have heard the miserable sophism that the best preparation for a sermon is knocking around the parish getting to know people. Of course a minister must know people, but he learns this by being a person. The first claim on his time is to seek to understand the mind of God through prayer and reading, and then secondly to prepare his sermon so that he has something to say when the people come to hear him. Otherwise they will not come, and who can blame them?

The second phenomenon is what may be called the flight from the parish ministry to special ministries and chaplaincies.

I learned this week that in one of the largest American theological colleges there is not a student who proposes to enter the ordinary parish ministry, but they are all keen to do one of these specialized helping ministries! And closely related is the fact that many ministers in the parishes are anxious to leave the parish ministry for some helping ministry. Yet these helping ministries are not ministries of the Word of God, though they doubtless provide opportunities for Christian witness just as any other job provides the opportunity from time to time for a man to witness to his faith. The essential Christian ministry is preaching the Word of God, as an evangelist or as a parish minister or both. Paul told Timothy that those ministers who labour in the Word and in teaching are especially worthy of double honour (*1 Tim. 5:17*). The reason is because the knowledge of God's Word is the basis of Christian faith and Christian fellowship. This is why the ministry of God's Word is so important and so honourable. It is the essential ministry. Without faithful, true and thoughtful preaching or teaching of God's Word, the Christian church will evaporate.

In the sixth chapter of Acts we have an interesting illustration of the supreme importance of the parish ministry of preaching and teaching the Word of God to the people of

God. The young Christian church in Jerusalem was growing in numbers, and the growing fellowship called for new patterns of service. Some members of the church were being neglected in the distribution of financial help. Now to assist in relieving the poverty of widows is a noble, loving, helping ministry, but the apostles, who had been called to the ministry of the Word of God, steadfastly refused to be drawn into this helping ministry or to allow their time to be absorbed by it. They said that they would leave it to the others to look after the widows; but that they themselves would concentrate on the essential ministry to which Christ had called them.

This ministry was twofold – preaching the Word as opportunity occurred (as on the Day of Pentecost and preaching in the synagogue) and teaching the Christian group from the Word of God, and prayer. We read in Acts 2:42 that the Christian converts continued in the apostles' teaching. It was this ministry of teaching that the apostles were determined to protect by refusing to allow other things, excellent though these were, to crowd it out. The reason is simple – the Word of God is vital for evoking Christian faith, so that if there is no Word of God preached, there will be no Christians, however busy people may be discharging these helping ministries. Faith comes by hearing and hearing by the Word of Christ, but how shall they hear, asked Paul, unless people preach? The Christian religion is a religion of faith – faith in Jesus as Lord; faith that God has raised him from the dead; faith that our Lord is coming again to be the judge and rewarder of those who seek him; faith that we will share in that coming kingdom. From this faith, this Christian world view, this recognition of Jesus as Lord, flows out Christian living in business and in the home. But this faith needs constant nurture from the Word of God, and God calls ministers of the Word to this task and they in turn need to give themselves to it and to the preparation which it requires if it is to be fulfilled. The Christian church is nothing other than fellowship in God, and this fellowship is deepened and maintained by the teaching of the Word of God by the minister. Without this teaching there can be no fellowship, that is, no church.

The ministry of the Word of God is a supernatural ministry. Its message is about supernatural things and its power depends on God's Spirit. If this ministry is to be persevered with to the end of the minister's life, he himself will need to be constantly revived in faith. Paul said in Romans I that he was not ashamed of the gospel as it was the power of God for salvation to everyone who believes; which showed that he recognized its supernatural character but that he also knew the temptation to be ashamed of it and to give it up. But he persevered and finished the course, as he put it, sustained by faith in God's promised reward, the crown of life.

To preach the Word of God requires faith on the preacher's part. Now this is not needed to the same extent in the helping ministries, as here you can see the good you are doing. In Acts 6 those who undertook the ministry of distributing money to the widows could see the joy on the widows' faces and hear their words of gratitude. They also had the satisfaction of healing the wound in the Christian fellowship. It was a real service and its fruits were plain. Yet the apostles refused to be drawn into this helping ministry, saying that they would give themselves to the ministry of the Word of God and prayer. This is a ministry in which the minister himself may often see little fruit. He will only maintain his ministry if his own faith in the supernatural world and in Christ as Lord remains bright. For this he needs to give time to Bible reading and prayer.

The apostles told the Christian church that they would continue steadfast in prayer and ministering the Word of God. Both are supernatural activities: prayer and preaching

God's Word. They both go together, for without prayer on the minister's part his own faith will grow dim, and his words will be without power. For it is the Spirit of God who applies the words to the hearts of the hearers to bring forth fruit for eternal life; and unless the minister's words arise from prayer they will not be the words which the Spirit can use, for they will not be the words which God gives.

Persevering in prayer is difficult, it takes time; and the preparation of the message takes time. If a minister believes he is called to the ministry of God, he would do well to follow the example of the apostles and curtail other activities, even though they are the excellent ones of helping other people in their need. That must be left to others who are not called to the ministry of the Word of God. But this line of action can only be followed if the minister himself is seized with the reality of the supernatural world and with God's supernatural purposes. He must be conscious that the gospel is the power of God to salvation to everyone who believes. And our Lord has a word of encouragement and warning. He said to his disciples, 'Who then is the faithful slave whom his Lord shall put over his household to give them their food in due season? Blessed is that servant whom his Lord when he comes shall find so doing. Truly I say to you he will set him over all that he has.' In addition to this promise of reward for faithfulness, Jesus added a warning to the servant who neglected the ministry to which God had appointed him. Jesus compared him to a human slave whom his master found negligent and unfaithful, who was severely scourged and rejected as a hypocrite; and Jesus added, 'There shall be weeping and gnashing of teeth' (*Matt. 24:51*).

6
Communicating the Gospel

The Christian church makes so slight an impact on the community, and so few people find any relevance in its message, that many of its spokesmen urge an overhaul of the methods of communication, that is, of getting the message across. And so we have chaplains appointed for this or for that; we have expensive programmes for the mass medium of television and we have the radical rewriting of the gospel in contemporary books which are professedly Christian.

It is, of course, right to be constantly reflecting on our methods; but the trouble may not be in the old methods, or in the message. It may be that the hearers do not want to hear. The problem of communication, so much talked about today, is not, in my judgment, the real problem. We do not have to reinterpret the Christian gospel but to reassert the gospel clearly and truly, believing it fully ourselves. This may not, of course, bring the results hoped for, because the hearers may not want to accept the gospel, and this is a problem which we must take to God in prayer.

Much modern talk about the problems of communication and presenting the gospel in a way acceptable to the modern man loses sight of the stubborn fact of the hardness of the human heart. It is natural that people do not see any relevance in the gospel, even when preached with clarity and persuasiveness, because their minds are spiritually blinded.

Jesus was a most able teacher; he knew the mind of God

perfectly and he was at one with his audience. His personality was winsome, his character perfect in its attractiveness. He spoke with authority and his message was accompanied with signs and miracles. In other words, Jesus was the ideal communicator; he had no need to overhaul his methods or his message – and yet what was the result? An almost complete failure to communicate the message in the sense of getting a favourable response from his hearers. It was not that there was any fault with the message or any fault with the teacher or his methods. The fault lay exclusively in the hardness of the hearts of the hearers.

Chapter 11 of Matthew records the failure. Jesus upbraided the communities in which he had spent his ministry because they took no notice. Their community life was quite unaffected by his message, or by his life lived amongst them, and so he warned these communities of their impending judgment. Naming the towns in which he worked, he warned, 'Woe unto Chorazin! Woe unto you, Bethsaida . . . and . . . you, Capernaum!' And the reason? Because they did not repent or take any notice of his ministry, even though it was accompanied by signs and miracles in the mighty works that he performed.

In Matthew 11:25 we find recorded our Lord's reaction to this indifference in those who heard, and it contains an interesting lesson for us, because Christians today are in a similar situation. We cannot claim, of course, to exercise the perfect ministry that Jesus exercised, but we are faced with the same disappointing indifference in those around us. Jesus would have experienced the same disappointment, for in his human life he underwent all our experiences. It is therefore worth noting our Lord's reaction to the situation. His reaction was threefold. First, he brought the matter to God in prayer. He recognized that God was sovereign in the situation and so he was able to thank God, even in the presence of disappointment and apparent lack of success.

His words are, 'I thank thee, O Father, Lord of heaven and earth, that thou hast hidden these things from the wise and prudent and revealed them unto babes; yea, Father, for so it was well-pleasing in thy sight'.

It remains true that God is Lord of heaven and earth. Nothing takes place apart from him. The success of our ministry does not depend on new methods of communication but on God's power granting or withholding, according to his wisdom, a knowledge of himself. Because God is sovereign, loving, wise and righteous, we are able to follow our Lord in giving God thanks always for everything, and not just sometimes for some things. The basic doctrine in Christianity is God's complete sovereignty and we must keep this in the front of our thoughts.

The second point in our Lord's reaction to the situation was a reaffirmation of the fundamental gospel facts, the very facts which had been rejected by his hearers. He said, 'All things have been delivered unto me of my Father: and no one knows the Father save the Son, and he to whom the Son wills to reveal him'. Jesus makes himself central in the history of humanity. He is central because, in Jesus, God has come into a new and permanent relationship to his creation. He has taken our nature and so given purpose and direction for the history of humanity. God's purpose for man is fellowship with him, fellowship based on forgiveness, made possible by Christ's death on the cross.

That purpose will be fulfilled when Christ returns and everyone will see that all power has been given to him. In the meantime, the Christian's service is to proclaim God's saving actions in Christ. This gives a supernatural view of human life – a dimension that is missing in most of our thinking today – and Christians are called upon, not to find new methods of communication so much as simply to insist, once more, on the reality of the supernatural – on God: his sovereignty, his coming into relationship with us in Christ and his purposes, still to be worked out in the future for the human race when Christ will reign and all that opposes itself to him will be judged and abolished.

Not only is Christ central in human history but he is central in our relationships with God. We cannot know God unless Christ reveals him to us. We cannot have fellowship with God apart from Christ. This is what Jesus affirmed in this verse, that 'no one knows the Father save he to whom the Son wills to reveal him'. We cannot bypass Christ in worshipping God. The reason is simple: all our relationships with God must be based on forgiveness; they cannot be based on our own worthiness, although we persist in thinking this to be so. Forgiveness comes to us through the death of Christ for sins on Calvary and we may enter into fellowship with God now only on the basis of forgiveness in Christ.

This is the Christian gospel. It is easily understood. It is not a question of finding new methods of communicating this gospel so much as needing the power of God to touch the hearts of the hearers so that they accept the very remarkable statements which they, at present, regard as untrue. It is not that the hearers cannot understand these statements but that they do not believe them, and in this situation the Christian church must follow the example of Jesus and simply repeat them, reaffirm them, and believe them itself.

We Christians must believe these supernatural facts of God – his judgment, forgiveness, the resurrection and the coming of Christ. For if we do not believe them, if we do not make them central in our own thinking and live by them, we will not get our hearers to believe them merely by changing our methods of communication. Unbelief is our problem – not faulty methods of communication – unbelief and sickly faith in our own minds and hearts and in our fellow church members. The problem of unbelief is not merely in secular society outside the church. Unbelief can only be taken away and faith strengthened by God, in response to prayer. We ought to pray for one another that God will increase our faith in the facts of the gospel.

We come to the third point of our Lord's reaction, which was simply to repeat the gospel invitation. 'Come unto me, all ye who are weary and heavy laden, and I will give you rest'. There is no other way. Jesus pointed out that the yoke of obedience which he invited men to accept was a yoke suited to their nature – 'My yoke is easy and my burden is light'. It is suited to our nature because we are made by God to conform to his image and character, and as we accept the yoke of Christ, that is, as we take him as our Lord and follow him as our example (or to put it in another way, obey him rather than ourselves), we will find that the life which he leads us to live is one which brings rest to our souls, because it conforms with God's purposes for us. The life of disobedience is the unhappy, awkward life; the life of obedience to Christ is the happy, restful life, the easy yoke.

So, then, as we Christians find ourselves in a similar position to that which our Lord faced at the end of his ministry – a general disregard of the gospel, and the community indifferent to it – we must follow his example in our response to the situation, refreshing our minds in the sovereignty of God. We must have recourse to him in prayer with thanksgiving, then reaffirming the great supernatural truths of God's relationship to us, in which Jesus Christ is central in history and religion, and reissuing his invitation, 'Come unto me . . . take my yoke upon you'. In inviting others, we must be sure that we have responded ourselves and accepted his lordship for our own lives and his values for our values.

7
Repentance: Preaching that is Out of Favour

It is always interesting to hear the first sermon a minister preaches in his pulpit, as this is often a key to what he regards as his most important message. And so it is of special interest to note what Jesus preached in his opening sermons. We read in Mark 1:14, 'Jesus came into Galilee, preaching the gospel of God, and saying, "The time is fulfilled and the kingdom of God is at hand; repent, and believe in the gospel"'. Or, as Matthew puts it, 'From that time Jesus began to preach, and to say, "Repent, for the kingdom of heaven is at hand"' (*Matt. 4:17*).

Later, when Jesus sent out his twelve apostles two by two on their preaching tour, he gave them the same message to proclaim, namely, that 'men should repent' (*Mark 6:12*); and Luke records that, after his resurrection, Jesus commissioned his disciples to preach repentance and the forgiveness of sins in his name to all the nations (*Luke 24:47*).

In the Acts of the Apostles we find the Christian missionaries carrying out this commission. Thus, on the day of Pentecost, Peter told the crowd assembled in Jerusalem, 'Repent and be baptized in the name of Jesus Christ for the forgiveness of your sins' (*Acts 2:38*). Later, Paul told the Ephesians that the message of his preaching was 'repentance

[38]

towards God and faith towards our Lord Jesus Christ' (*Acts 20:21*). Throughout the New Testament we find the same call to repentance and promise of forgiveness through Christ. This is the Christian gospel – the gospel of forgiveness – and repentance is the gateway.

Repentance means a turning towards God. Everybody needs to repent because none of us honours God as we should. Almost everyone believes in God, but few honour him as God, or hallow his name in thought and life. Even the best of us do not do this as we should and that is why we need forgiveness if we are to be acquitted in the judgment of God. Quite apart from the many wrong acts and thoughts which we fall into, we all come short of the most obvious obligation of acknowledging God and being properly thankful to the God whose existence we admit. We need to repent and be forgiven if we are to escape the judgment of God and be restored to his fellowship. The Christian message is that there is forgiveness for those who will turn towards God. God in his love has provided the way of forgiveness through the death of our Saviour, who bore our sins in his body on the cross.

Since God-forgetfulness is the radical sin of mankind, repentance and forgiveness is the only message that meets the situation. We may take this New Testament message of repentance and forgiveness as the yardstick, to measure and test what is being preached in our pulpits, or is being taught by our missionaries, or what we ourselves believe. For example, what place do repentance and forgiveness have in the message of our churches? Or in our books of theology? How prominent is the message of repentance and forgiveness in our modern religious literature? This is the test; but is a test which many books fail.

We may not be aware that we need to repent and be forgiven. But the basic sin which makes salvation by our merits impossible is our failure to love and honour God with all our heart, as we ought to since he is our Creator. Jesus said, 'You cannot serve God and mammon' (*Matt. 6:24*) and yet most of us are endeavouring to do this. Not that we wish to serve mammon entirely, but we want to serve God *and* mammon. But this is impossible, for God is the true and holy God and we must honour him and serve him absolutely and completely, or we do not honour him or serve him at all. In this matter each of us needs to be daily repentant and daily seek God's forgiveness.

The call for repentance in response to the gospel of forgiveness has always been the keynote of every great Christian revival. Repentance depends on our realization of who God is – the true and living God – and the recognition that we cannot serve him so long as we have other objectives – whether happiness or security or whatever it is – existing in our minds as objectives to be sought for in their own right, alongside the objective of serving God. Because we all have these insignificant objectives which are not directly related to the mind of God, we need to repent and be forgiven.

The message of repentance is out of favour in many Christian circles these days. A symptom of this is the opinion that a person may find God in any of the great religions of the world. At the Commonwealth Day Service, held on March 11, 1991 in Westminster Abbey, London, in the presence of the Queen and the Prince of Wales, Muslim, Jewish, Hindu, Sikh and Buddhist leaders read or chanted from the sacred texts of their faiths. This is the culmination of influences long in existence among the churches. A leading missionary speaker at the Anglican Toronto Congress in 1963 put Islam, Buddhism and other heathen religions alongside Christianity as being true reflections of God's revelation of himself. I quote from his address:

We should be able to insist that God was speaking in that cave on the hill outside Mecca (that is, to Mohammed), that God brought illumination to the man who once sat under the bo tree (that is, to Buddha).

He went on:

> God speaks to me in my newspaper as well as in the Bible, he seeks me out in the theatre, in the novel, in art, as well as in the Holy Communion.

This modern view, which blurs the uniqueness of relationship with Jesus Christ as the way of salvation, is not confined to the Protestant denominations but is affirmed by the Second Vatican Council of the Roman Catholic Church. In the Declaration on non-Christian religions, paragraph 3, the Second Vatican Council stated:

> Moslems adore the one God, living and subsisting in himself, merciful and all powerful, the Creator of heaven and earth, who has spoken to men; they take pains to submit wholeheartedly to his inscrutable decrees just as Abraham . . . submitted to God. Though they do not acknowledge Jesus as God they revere him as a prophet.

This statement leaves no room for the message of repentance and forgiveness. The Muslims appear to be on the right track, only needing to go further, rather than to turn round and obtain forgiveness for following a false religion. The statement blurs the sharp distinction between a man-made religion, which puts Mohammed on a higher level than the Son of God, and the religion of the Bible, which teaches that God became man in order to provide the only way of salvation for men. The Council's view fits in with modern ideas but it is diametrically opposed to the words of Jesus, 'I am the way, the truth, and the life: no one comes to the Father but by me' (*John 14:6*), and 'no one knows the Father save the Son, and he to whom the Son wills to reveal him' (*Matt. 11:27*).

[41]

The Second Vatican Council repeated its teaching in the Constitution of the Church published in November 1964, paragraph 16:

The plan of salvation also includes . . . the Moslems . . .

and it goes on:

. . . those also can attain to salvation who strive by their deeds to do his will as it is known to them through the dictates of conscience.

By these words the Council affirms that the sincere pagan who knows nothing of Christ may be saved by striving to do what is right. The message of Buddha to his disciples was, 'Strive without ceasing'. This is not the Christian message which is 'repent and believe the gospel' – the gospel of forgiveness of sins in the name of Christ. This modern message omits the call for repentance and the offer of forgiveness, for where is the place of forgiveness if people can be saved by striving to follow their own conscience?

A religion of salvation by striving is self-centred and tends to pride; but salvation through forgiveness glorifies God for his grace, and leads to humility. Salvation through merit which results from successful striving and salvation through forgiveness have nothing in common. During past centuries the Roman Catholic Church held both these doctrines in an uneasy union and taught that forgiveness was obtained through the sacraments, and that to use the sacraments was an act of merit. But in the statements of the Second Vatican Council, the need of forgiveness is but mentioned and merit alone is the way of salvation. God's grace has been cheapened. Christ's death has become merely a preliminary not requiring mention, instead of being the very centre of salvation – as in the early church, when Peter told the rulers of Jerusalem, 'In none other is there salvation, neither is there any other name under heaven wherein we must be saved' than the name of Jesus Christ (*Acts 4:12*).

Jesus is God's answer to man's sin, to man's neglect and dishonouring of his Creator. To be saved we must be united to Jesus, by acknowledging him as Lord. No sinner can be saved merely by striving. There must be a complete about-turn, a repentance, a return to God and an asking for and obtaining of forgiveness, which comes through being made one with Christ.

Tested by this unchanging message of the Bible, many modern theologies come short of the truth. Let us see to it that we ourselves are repentant, and base our hope of salvation, not on our own strivings or the quality of our life, but only on God's forgiveness in Jesus Christ.

8
Masculine Terminology concerning the Deity and the Consequences for Congregational Life

Masculine pronouns are consistently used throughout the Bible in reference to God. There are no exceptions. Masculine terms are used to describe God, such as 'father', 'husband', 'king', 'lord'. Moreover, our Lord Jesus Christ in his incarnation became a man.

The question is whether this uniformity is accidental. The ancient world was well aware of female deities; they were sometimes the chief deity of the worshipper. The consistency of biblical usage cannot therefore be explained as accidental, and for similar reasons it is improbable that it should be merely sociological, reflecting the customs of the day. If the reason is theological, that is, if it is based on God's attributes and his relation to the world, this is the complete explanation of the consistent biblical usage, and it should control our own usage and thought.

Three attributes of God are revealed in Scripture which are relevant to this question: his authority; his power and omnipotence; and his creative initiative and causality.

God created humanity as men and women: and as they stand before him, men and women are absolutely equal. They are equidistant from him, and they enjoy equal access to him, so that in Christ 'there is neither male nor female' (*Gal. 3:28*). The gender distinction in human life has no relevance to our relationship with God.

In the created world in general, men and women are equal, and the different functions and jobs they discharge in society will be determined by their native abilities and their opportunities, except of course in such societies where custom improperly restricts these opportunities unequally. It is true that men as a whole have masculine characteristics while women as a whole have feminine characteristics and that these characteristics will determine the general style of society. But there will always be exceptions in that some women will have characteristics more common to men and vice versa. It would be wrong to bar a woman from occupying any position in society for which her gifts and opportunities fit her.

But turning from the general social life, where men and women are equal, to those relationships of men and women in which the polarity of the sexes has significance, namely marriage and the home, we see both in nature and in Scripture distinctions which are never confused. Here the roles of male and female are quite distinct, cannot be reversed or interchanged and are not the same.

It is in fact this area of relationship to one another which gives meaning to the bifurcation of the sexes and which controls the masculine terminology for God. For in the relationship of man and women in sex, that is to say in

marriage, it is seen that God has imposed the pattern of his
relationship to creation on the male in a primary way.
Considered individually as members of society at large, both
men and women reflect the divine attributes of authority,
power and creativity. Both have authority and dignity, both
have power, and both have creative initiative. But considered
in their relationship, that is to say in the polarity of the sexes,
the male displays greater authority (if only in the depth of his
voice), greater power (if only in the strength of his biceps)
and clearly his sole physiological initiative in procreation,
that is, in creative initiative and causality.

The impress of this definite pattern is found only in the
institution of marriage. There is no necessity for it to be
projected into the ad hoc institutions that arise in society, so
that the extension of the male primacy into all these
institutions is illegitimate. This, for example, was the
mistake John Knox made in his book *The First Blast of the
Trumpet Against the Monstrous Regiment* [i.e. rule] *of Women*.

The relationship of marriage is modelled by the Creator on
his own relationship to creation. In marriage the husband
reflects Christ; his spouse reflects the church (*Eph. 5*).
Consequently it is not surprising that the Bible affirms the
primacy of male to female in the marriage relationship. Thus
man was made first, then woman (*Gen. 2:21, 22; 1 Tim.
2:13*). Thus also man was made, then woman was made for
him, not vice versa (*Gen. 2:18; 1 Cor. 11:9*). And woman was
made from him (*1 Cor. 11:8*).

Paul affirms that the head of every man is Christ and the
head of every woman is the man, and the head of Christ is
God (*1 Cor. 11:3*); man is the glory and image of God and the
woman is the glory of man (*1 Cor. 11:7*). The woman is the
weaker of the two (*1 Peter 3:7*) and is the less suitable for
leadership (*1 Tim. 2:11–14*). This is accentuated by the
relationship of husband and wife as a consequence of fallen
human nature (*Gen. 3:16c*). It is important to recognize that

this differentiation of function within marriage does not imply any inferiority. The Bible is absolutely clear on this (*I Cor. II:II, I2*); nor is there any reason why it should be carried over into ordinary social relationships outside the marriage bond or the Christian congregation, both of which are reflections of Christ's relation to the church in a way that the relationships of secular society are not.

Thus when God is spoken of in Scripture, or when he became incarnate in human form, he is masculine because he displays the male attributes par excellence as these are distinct in the male/female polarity. To creation at large, God is neither masculine nor feminine. To mankind he is masculine (though the Scriptures do not affirm that he is male but use the masculine pronouns) and in Jesus he became incarnate as a man.

In addition to the three divine attributes of authority, power and creativity, God is also love. The human experience of love is in accordance with the modes of the different sexes, and in describing God's love for his people, he is consistently described as the Father, the Husband and the Saviour of the body. In Ephesians 3:15 Paul affirms that all fatherhood is derived from and takes its character from the Fatherhood of God.

The consistent masculine terminology used of God is thus theological and not merely sociological.

The consequence of the masculine terminology for God for the organization of human relationships depends on whether that relationship is organized according to the family, or is an ad hoc association in society at large. The family in its organization is closely related to and depends on the polarity of the sexes, and therefore it reflects the relationship of men and women in their sexual relationship in which the headship and primacy is in the husband.

The organization of the Christian congregation should reflect that of the family, for it is not an ad hoc association or social grouping in which masculinity and femininity have no special part to play. Husband and wife are the microcosm of Christ and his people (*Eph.* 5:22–23). The congregation is the local expression of this same relationship of Christ and his people. Hence the fellowship of the family and that of the congregation are closely united. Both are expressions of God's relationships in a way that other human institutions are not.

We may assume, therefore, that God will not organize the fellowship of the congregation to contravene the divine ordering of the fellowship of the family, for the family is modelled on the divine relationship of God and his people, of Christ and his church, of which the local congregation is the expression. And this assumption is confirmed by the explicit statements of Scripture.

The family and the congregation stand together over against all other human organizations as they alone are both expressions of God's relationship to his people. God's pattern for the organization of the congregation will not contradict, but will be found to be in conformity with the pattern of the organization of the family. This is the explanation why Scripture so clearly forbids wives to rule in the congregation for they are not to rule their husbands in the family (*1 Tim.* 3:4,12).

When we think of the work and ministry of deacons, priests and bishops in the Church of England as it is in actual fact discharged today, there may seem to be no reason why women should not be ordained to discharge any or all of these three ministries.

A minister's life is very variegated. His most conspicuous activity is the conducting of services. Before electronics had reached their present perfection it might have been argued that by nature women had not been given the equipment of the larynx to make them suitable leaders of public services or readers of the lessons or public speakers in any large gathering; but this is no longer the case since the perfection of amplifying systems. Furthermore, many women are excellent counsellors, much better than some men. A woman is as able to preside at a parish council or a synod as is a man, and so one could go on. There would be no objection to a woman consecrating a bishop, ordaining clergy, confirming young people, baptizing, taking the service of Holy Communion, marrying young couples or burying the dead, if these actions could be considered in themselves *apart from the context of the congregation*. Women already are very active in visiting from house to house as district visitors, in visiting in hospitals, in teaching in schools and in Sunday schools. What remains, it may be asked, of clerical or episcopal functions as we know them in practice today, which is such that women are excluded by nature from being commissioned to undertake them?

However, the question is not finally settled by observing what ministers do these days. For it may well be that ministers are not doing what they ought to be doing. The question is to be decided, not by observing what goes on today, but exclusively by biblical principles. For these ministries are spiritual offices and take their character from the Word of God, although they may have had added to them over the centuries all sorts of other activities which are good in themselves but not the essential activities of these ministries. These ministries are ministries 'in the church', that is, in the congregation. It is there that God has placed them (*1 Cor. 12:28; Titus 1:5*), and they take their character from the character of the congregation, and the congregation in turn takes its character from the principle on which it is formed, so that the role of the minister can be understood only in relation to the role of the congregation.

The New Testament congregation was formed of people who were living by the hope of Christ. Their whole lives were oriented to this hope. Very largely, they would have come

[49]

from homes where the whole household had accepted Jesus as Lord and were looking for his kingdom. Not only would they as individuals be engaged in Christian fellowship daily (*Acts 2:46*), but when they came together for wider fellowship in the local congregation, they would come as households. And the heads of the households would naturally take positions of pre-eminence. It is from this group of household heads that the Christian ministers are to be drawn, according to the New Testament. Deacons and presbyters are both required to be heads of Christian homes who conduct their homes so that they reflect a Christian character. 'Appoint elders in every city . . . having children that believe, who are not accused of riot or unruly' (*Titus 1:5, 6*). 'The bishop [minister] must be . . . one that rules well his own house, having his children in subjection with all gravity; if a man knows not how to rule his own house, how shall he take care of the church of God?' (*1 Tim. 3:2, 4, 5*). 'Let deacons be husbands of one wife ruling their children and their own houses well' (*1 Tim. 3:12*).

The head of a Christian home has authority. Authority is derived from responsibility, and the responsibility of the parental head is to bring up his children in the fear and nurture of the Lord. This is no new responsibility in the Christian dispensation, for the godly parent in the Old Testament times was commanded 'to make the things of God known unto thy children and thy children's children' (*Deut. 4:9*). Every opportunity was to be taken: 'thou shalt teach them diligently unto thy children, and shalt talk of them when thou sittest in thine house, and when thou walkest by the way, and when thou liest down, and when thou risest up' (*Deut. 6:7*) – or, as we would say, 'in the evening, on holiday, when driving the car, at bedtime and at breakfast'. Godly instruction, formal and informal, is the obligation of parents.

As I have said, the local congregation takes its character from the family congregation, the 'church in the house' (*Acts 2:46; Rom. 16:5, etc.*). It must not then conduct its affairs in a way that overturns the structures of the homes which go to make up that congregation and on which the congregation is based. Paul enjoins that congregational leaders are to be fathers. Is this a basic principle or merely a cultural pattern? There is no doubt that the Bible is clear that as a basic principle the headship of the home rests in the father. In Genesis 3:16 the wife is told that her husband shall rule over her. It is true that this is part of the consequence of sin; nevertheless, even in the redeemed community it remains a true principle, in the same way as obedience to the state (another consequence of the fall) is binding on the redeemed. Christian wives are frequently enjoined (and not only by Paul) to be in subjection to their own husbands. Just as husbands are told to love and honour their wives, so wives are told to obey, to reverence and to fear their husbands (*Eph. 5:22–24, 33; 1 Pet. 3:1, 2*). Of course, there is no servility in this hierarchical order. 'Lording it' is as vile an attitude on the husband's part as status seeking is on the part of the other.

Scripture is clear that there is a hierarchy in Christ – God, Christ, husband, wife, in that order (*1 Cor. 11:3*). It is impossible to discount this passage as merely reflecting first-century culture, though the consequence of this principle will vary in different cultures. In Paul's time the consequence was that women should be veiled in public. In our own culture this is not the consequence that we would draw. Paul reinforces this principle of order in the home, and as a consequence in the congregation, by recalling the sequence in creation. The husband is the image and glory of God; the wife the glory of her husband. The man is created independently but the woman not only from the man but also for the man (*1 Cor. 11:7–11*). These statements remain true in every culture since they are derived from the biblical narratives of the creation of men and women. Everyone is equal in God's sight – this is the meaning of Galatians 3:28. Both man and woman were created in the image of God; but everyone has not the same function. In the home there is a headship and the headship is that of the father – and this should be reflected in the Christian congregation.

We are challenged by the present situation to return to a more biblical organization of our congregations, and if we were to do this we would find that ordained women would be a problem. If women have no authority in the home over their husbands, then they ought not to have the authority in the church in the presence of their husbands (this is an equally clear principle in Scripture). Those who lead in the church are those who lead in the home; this again is a clear principle in Scripture. We have got away from this principle but we should be moving to return to it, rather than modifying Scripture as a result of the spirit of the age. To know better than the Bible is fatal. This was Adam's sin in the Garden. That sin is still with us, both within the Christian home as well as outside it. We must be on our guard; there is no future for the Christian gospel amongst those who know better than the Bible. The clear principles of the Bible must guide all our activities and in particular our activities of Christian association. Consequently, it is not possible to commission women as leaders and governors in the congregation (*Rom. 12:8; 1 Cor. 12:28, etc.*) for such officers have the duty to lay the Word of God authoritatively on the consciences of those who are present. This would mean, if they were women, ruling their own husbands, in direct contradiction of the will of God (*cf. 1 Pet. 3:1*). The relationship between the sexes required by God in families is not to be turned topsy-turvy in his congregation.

Scripture is absolutely clear that women are not to rule in the congregation or to engage in teaching which involves ruling. The fact that no-one admonishes anybody in the modern congregation, nor rules another's conscience through the Word of God, is only a condemnation of our modern ways and is no justification for departing further from the biblical norm by appointing women to the obsolescent position of ruling and so effectively excluding the possibility of its revival and return to its biblical function. There are other ministries which women fulfill well, such as the important ministry of encouragement. There is also a very large teaching ministry for women – it extends over more than half humanity – but it is to be confined to the teaching of women and is not to be exercised in the congregation in a way that would imply dominion over men (*I Tim. 2:12*).

More attention needs to be given to encouraging and training women to teach in their own homes and for the older women to teach the younger women how to run Christian homes (*Titus 2:3–4*).

The home is the basis of society. We must recognize the hierarchy that God has ordained, though we must ensure that this is not in any way a hierarchy of lording it on the one hand and of servility on the other. And we should endeavour to bring our congregations round to the place where they are in fact the meetings of Christian families, *meeting as families*.

From the above it should be clear that these scriptural directives are binding on us because they are theological and not merely sociological. They spring from the created order and not from changing social customs.

Certain important consequences for congregational life follow. The congregation should nourish the spiritual life and fellowship of the family. For example, up to half-a-dozen leaders should be chosen in each congregation whose first ministry should be to minister to families, i.e. to fathers and mothers, to encourage them to ensure that their home is a school of Christ. Fathers and mothers should spend an hour a day teaching their young children the Christian faith and its consequences for living. They will never persevere in this unless encouraged to do so by the leaders visiting them in their homes to enquire and exhort them along this line. It is a task too large for the full-time minister single-handed. A large part of his time will be devoted to preparation for preaching, for unless his preaching and teaching reaches a proper level of fulness of content, fathers and mothers will never be able to keep on teaching their children day by day, and unless homes have this depth of Christian knowledge and commitment, congregations will remain weak and shallow and evaporating.

9
'The Church' and 'The Denominations'

The important word 'church' is used in current language with at least six different meanings. It is used for a building, a denomination, or a profession. But interestingly enough it is seldom used in its basic New Testament meaning. We should be on our guard lest what is true of the word in one of its meanings is transferred to its use in another meaning. In particular we need to be on guard lest the aura of glory which surrounds its New Testament meaning is used to heighten loyalty to institutions other than the New Testament church.

In the New Testament the word 'church' always means 'a gathering' or 'an assembly'. Acts 19 shows it was not a technical ecclesiastical word, for in verse 32 Luke used it of the gathering of the mob in the theatre in Ephesus, and in verse 39 of the regular political assembly of the citizens. In the Old Testament the two Hebrew equivalents of the Greek *ekklēsia* are applied to the Old Testament people of God, especially when that people is conceived of as assembling or gathering; for example when gathered at Mount Sinai for the giving of the law by God, or later on Mount Zion where all Israel was required to assemble three times a year. The usual English equivalents of the Hebrew are 'congregation' and 'assembly', but Stephen in Acts 7 used the word 'church' (i.e. *ekklēsia*) of this Old Testament congregation of God. In the New Testament the Christian church is the fulfilment of the Old Testament assembly. Jesus Christ is its constituent.

Just as in Exodus 19:4, 5, God is said to have gathered his people around himself at Mount Sinai, and as later they regularly gathered at his command around his dwelling place on Mount Zion, so Christ gathers his people around himself as their Shepherd. He gathers them through the preaching of the gospel: 'The Lord added day by day those that were being saved' (*Acts 2:47*). It is Christ who builds his church (*Matt. 16:18*). He calls his sheep into one flock around him, whether near or far off (*John 10:16; Acts 2:39*).

The Epistle to the Hebrews makes clear that the assembly, or church, which Christ is building now is primarily a heavenly assembly. In Hebrews 12:18–24 the writer contrasts the assembly of which his readers are members with the Old Testament assembly of the people of God. That earlier assembly was gathered around God on Mount Sinai but the present assembly into which Christian believers have been gathered is on the Heavenly Zion, the City of the Living God. This assembly is described as 'the church of the firstborn enrolled in heaven', that is, the gathering of God's true people ('The first born are mine', *Exod. 13:2*). This is the essential Christian church and it is gathered round Christ where he now is. Our membership of this assembly or church is not some future hope but is a present reality, 'You have come . . .'. The Book of Revelation gives us several glimpses of this heavenly assembly around Christ (*Rev. 7:9; 14:1*). Christ is now primarily to be thought of as in heaven (*Col. 3:1; 1 Pet. 3:22; Acts 3:21; Acts 7:55*).

Since Christ is now in heaven, it is there that the New Testament thinks of him as building his church, because the church of Christ is the assembly which he calls into being around himself. This church or assembly round Christ is a present, not merely a future reality, and we are to think of ourselves as already members of it, assembled with him in Heaven. This is the primary reference of the word 'church' in the New Testament (*Matt. 16:18; Eph. 5:25*). This is the church affirmed in the Nicene Creed, 'I believe in one Holy Catholic Apostolic church.' Its principle of unity is the fact that Christ has assembled it around himself. It is logically impossible for him to assemble two churches around himself, for Christ is to be thought of as in one place only, that is, in heaven, if we are to use biblical imagery, which is the only imagery available. This gathering or church is holy, because it is God's; it has been called out by God for himself. It may also be called holy because its members are holy, not only in status but also in character (*1 John 3:2*). It is catholic because the gospel is no longer confined to the literal seed of Abraham, but rather Christ is gathering into his church 'out of every nation and of all tribes and peoples and tongues'. It is apostolic because it is founded on the apostles, that is to say, Christ's commissioned missionaries who founded the church by preaching the gospel of Christ. It is the heavenly church which is apostolic (*Rev. 21:14*) as well as catholic, holy and indivisibly one.

We are called into membership of this one church of Christ by the preaching of the gospel. As a consequence of membership of Christ's church there is a duty on Christians to assemble in local gatherings. This duty was not so obvious to the early Christians that they did not need to be exhorted not to forsake the assembling of themselves together (*Heb. 10:25*). The letters of Ignatius of Antioch are notorious for their constant repetition of the duty of Christians to assemble together rather than to worship God on their own. These exhortations confirm that in its primary meaning in the New Testament, the word 'church' refers to that heavenly assembly which Christ is gathering. Every New Testament Christian was vividly conscious of belonging to the church as he awaited his Lord from heaven. The fact that these early Christians nevertheless required exhortation to assemble together locally shows that their concept of the church of Christ, of which they all knew themselves to be members, was in essence other than the local group.

Though a derived and not a primary use, nevertheless the most frequent use of the word in the New Testament is of the local gathering of Christians. These local gatherings, whether in Corinth or in the cities of Galatia, or in Jerusalem, were manifestations of the one church of Christ. Christ had gathered them, and he himself was present according to his promise where two or three had met together in his name. Thus they were gathered round Christ through his Spirit, and consequently nothing was lacking for a complete church of Christ. They were never spoken of as part of Christ's church because they were Christ's church, gathered by him round himself at a certain time in a certain place. They were manifestations of the heavenly church of which every true member of the local church was at that very time a member. It is a grave mistake, common in current theology, to reverse the order and to think of Christ's universal church as made up by adding together the total membership of the local churches whether backwards through time or extensively over the earth's surface. It is worth noting that Ignatius who was the first to use the term 'the catholic church', applied it to the gathering of Christians around Jesus. 'Where Jesus is, there is the Catholic Church' (*ad Smyrn. 8*). Jesus is in heaven. That is how the New Testament consistently described him and that is how the early Christians thought of him from whence also they were waiting for him to be their Saviour (*Phil. 3:20*). The longer recension of Ignatius' letter makes it even clearer that the catholic church is that heavenly gathering 'from every nation and from all tribes, peoples and tongues, standing . . . before the Lamb' (*Rev. 7:9; cf. Matt. 24:31*). The longer recension paraphrases, 'where Jesus is, there is the catholic church,' by 'where Jesus is, there the heavenly army is drawn up at the side of its commander' (*cf. Rev. 19:14*).

The catholic church is indivisibly one, for Christ has only one heavenly gathering around himself of which all believers are members (*Heb. 12:18ff.*). It is holy because it is God's (*Num. 8:13*). It is apostolic because the apostles are its foundation stones (*Rev. 21:14*). The heavenly church is the one holy catholic church of the creeds. It is affirmed as an article of faith because it is not an object of sight. It is the spiritual fellowship which Christians experience in their spirits with Christ and with one another in Christ. As the Apostles' Creed adds, it is the communion of saints, that is, the fellowship of believers.

This heavenly church and this spiritual fellowship gives expression to itself spontaneously in local gatherings, for the Spirit of Christ in each draws all together to meet with Christ in each other. The visible church is the local church. As Article 19 of the Thirty-Nine Articles says: 'The visible church of Christ is a congregation of faithful [i.e., believing] men [i.e. people] wherein the pure word of God is preached and the sacraments duly administered . . .'. It is only in the local congregation that the Word of God is preached and the sacraments administered. It is only the assembled congregation that is visible. The preaching of the pure Word of God ensures that the congregation is composed of believers. Others – except, perhaps, for a small handful – will be converted or leave.

The heavenly church is visible in its expression, the local congregation, and in the visibility of the Christian character of its members. Outsiders will notice it – 'see how these Christians love one another'. The love of the congregation for fellow Christians will extend to love of other congregations of Christ's people. There will be fellowship in Christ within the congregation, created by the indwelling Spirit of God in the hearts and lives of all, and there will be fellowship between congregations, through the impulse and leading of the same Spirit. It is impossible to discover in the New Testament any other link or relationship of the local churches one with the other than this invisible bond of mutual love of the members one for the other.

The local churches come into being as their members are joined to Christ. These local churches will never be visibly one assembly until the Second Coming. Then, when Christ is manifested, the church will be seen to be united around him; and Paul in 2 Thessalonians 2:1 speaks of this quite correctly as our 'gathering together' around him in the air.

These days, structures naturally arise to assist the fellowship within congregations and to assist the fellowship between congregations. When there are more than one of these structures in any area, they are normally called denominations. But whether one or many, or whatever their name, these structures are not churches or part of the church. They are 'parachurch' organizations for they exist alongside the churches to facilitate fellowship within and between churches, each one of which is a full and true visible expression of the one holy catholic heavenly church, the fellowship round Christ of all his saints (*Heb. 12:22–24*), for Christ is present and so are his people in each local church. Nothing more is needed for a full expression of the gathering, or church, of Christ.

This parachurch organization must not exercise the duties of the congregation on behalf of the congregation for this takes away the responsibilities of the congregation and so weakens instead of strengthens its fellowship. In particular, a denomination must be careful not to exercise jurisdiction within the congregation, for it is outside the congregation and not in personal fellowship with those in dispute, so its jurisdiction may well lead to schism within the congregation and obscure the visible unity of the church.

Nowadays, denominationalism is greatly strengthened by the centralized service structure which has been built up to serve denominationally-linked churches. This service structure very frequently has control of the denominational property and so is able to apply effective sanctions over the local congregation and its ministers. Denominationalism depends very largely for its continued existence nowadays on property ownership. If property were not owned on trust for the use of the denominational 'church,' denominational edges would soon be blurred, for it is the continuance of this church trust property which perpetuates the separate denominations when the original *raison d'être* for their separate existence has ceased. Perhaps the most serious danger which the denominational groupings of Christian congregations presents is that such groupings provide a focal point for loyalty. For many members, especially for the more carnal members, the denomination replaces the true centre of loyalty which a Christian assembly should have, namely Christ who gathers his assembly together. Thus nowadays we witness Christians assembling, both locally and on a world-wide scale, on the ground of their denominational allegiance, and the issue is confused by the fact that invariably the denomination is called 'the church,' as though Christ who assembles his church were also the one who is assembling the denominational gathering.

A denomination is seen in its best light when viewed from the service which it provides for the local Christian assemblies. Thus it normally provides expert advice and mediation in many areas; it provides training colleges for the ministers; it provides financial facilities for the purchase of congregational amenities, such as a church building to assemble in, a residence for the minister and such like. It may also provide a channel for supporting missionaries in their ministry overseas, and in this respect it has a New Testament prototype in the aid the Philippians provided Paul with for the full-time exercise of his ministry. When viewed as a service organization, the union of denominations may be beneficial as leading to greater efficiency, so long as this

[61]

efficiency is not purchased at the cost of truth or liberty. Thus often the union of denominations is an object to be encouraged, though it is unwarranted to think that such union in itself is a spiritual objective which Christians are under obligation to strive for.

Denominational organization increases the influence of the denomination in the community. Some denominations, specially those who give high-sounding titles to their office-bearers, are more effective than others in securing influence in the community. But it remains true that influence secured by denominational organization is worldly influence rather than the influence which arises from the power of the gospel, and so it may fail to advance God's glory. God's purposes are not advanced by pressure groups, but by prayer, preaching and Christian living and suffering. A strong denominational structure enables a 'denominational witness' to be maintained in areas where otherwise the congregation would die out. Thus when there is a prolonged failure to preach the gospel with the consequential absence of the Spirit of God at work, it is only the existence of a church building, parochial structure, parsonage and stipend which keeps a congregation in existence. It is normally assumed that such continuity of the 'church's' witness, even though more or less a dead witness, is a good thing, and to God's glory. But the assumption is highly questionable.

'Parallel denominationalism' may be defined as more than one denomination having churches in the same locality. The blessing that parallel denominationalism brings with it is liberty of conscience. A single denomination has always been a persecuting denomination and has maintained its monopoly only by persecution. It is well to remember this as we witness the present efforts under the umbrella of the ecumenical movement to bring about an amalgamation of denominational structures. Amalgamation through negotiation will never completely succeed nor be permanently monolithic without the aid of persecution. The old-fashioned method of burning at the stake is for the time being at least out of favour, but there are other forms of persecution to suppress liberty of conscience. Moreover the efforts of the ecumenical movement in aiming at the unification of denominational structures are directed towards achieving an irrelevancy, and if successful will accentuate the temptations of denominationalism in proportion to the success in creating a big denomination. The real way forward is a return to the ancient pattern of mutual acceptance of one another without negotiating a 'union scheme' of the denominations to which the local churches happen to belong. The restrictive character of the denominational link-up should be weakened by gladly allowing and indeed encouraging, congregations and individual Christians to be in fellowship with each other across the denominational barriers. Enlarging the link-up by denominational amalgamation, or 'church union', as it is called, may only strengthen its exclusiveness.

Instead of elaborate denominational amalgamation, what is needed as a first step is denominational simplification by handing back to the congregations those functions and responsibilities which they had in the New Testament and the early centuries. Then it would not be difficult to unite into unity of fellowship churches in such simplified denominational structures.

Denominations are called 'churches' and this nomenclature misleads many into thinking that they are part of the one holy catholic apostolic church. But the denomination is not a church in as much as the denomination never gathers. A gathering is the only meaning of the word 'church' in the Old and New Testaments. The church building is also called a church. This is the most common use of the word. But no-one confuses the building with the church of Christ. The difference is clear in English-language usage. 'To go to church' means to go to the local gathering of the church. 'To go to the church' means to go to the church building. The church building is a physical structure to facilitate the fellowship of the church by keeping out the wind and rain. It has no other purpose. The denomination is an organizational structure to facilitate the fellowship of the church with Christians in other churches. To call the denomination a church is strictly inaccurate and in further-ance of clarity of thought ought to be dropped and the word denomination always substituted. For it would be of great assistance to the clarity of theological thinking if the word 'church' were restricted in its use once more to the church which Christ assembles around himself in heaven and to the local manifestation in time and place of this one church of Christ. When we speak of the 'church' as a shorthand term, to describe all our Christian brethren at present living in the world (as in the phrase, 'the church militant here on earth') or when we use it for a denomination, as the Church of England, or the Presbyterian Church, these are non-bibilical senses; and it is here that the confusion arises, because we bring over into these modern non-biblical uses the theology of glory which applies to the New Testament church.

All this is not to say that Independency is the right Christian concept for the churches. Interdependence, not independence is the true Christian relationship. Con-gregations should be in fellowship with one another. They should not act independently of other congregations. Christ-ian fellowship should know no limits. Such is the fellowship of heaven and the limits we know in our earthly fellowship ought simply to be the limits of human life and not limits of attitude.

Denominational structures may assist the interdependence of congregations. For the denominational structure exists to facilitate this wider fellowship beyond the congregation as opportunities arise for it to be expressed. It links congrega-tions with one another. It creates and provides facilities for the congregations in matters concerning fellowship, such as suggested liturgies, finance for buildings, superannuation for its ministers and opportunity from time to time for fellowship with congregations drawn from a wider area than the locality, and so on. Such links are a natural creation of the fellowship of the Spirit of God.

The denomination's officers have a ministry which is common to all Christians, that is, to help, advise, encourage, exhort, and serve the congregation and its members. A denomination should not apply sanctions to the congregation or to any of its members beyond the sanction of severing its links of fellowship with that congregation. Coercion destroys fellowship. On its part a congregation should be free to sever its links with a denomination without penalty, for example, without loss of the property it uses. Coercion is contrary to the character and rule of God and to fellowship in Christ.

Christians may affirm that in their judgment the structure and doctrinal basis of association of the denomination to which they belong does not contravene the Word of God. But to assert that the denomination, *per se*, as distinct from the regenerate Christians associated with it, is part of Christ's church is to attempt to combine concepts utterly disparate. Christ's church is certainly visible on earth, (for invisible gatherings on earth would be a contradiction) but it is not to be identified with the confederations called denominations.

10
The Joy of Ministry

In Luke's Gospel, chapter 10, verse 20, we read 'Howbeit in this rejoice not, that the spirits are subject to you; but rejoice that your names are written in heaven'.

This verse comes at the end of a short passage reporting our Lord's words to the seventy disciples on their return from the ministry on which he had sent them. They came back full of joy in the success of their ministry. Jesus had sent them into the towns and villages which he was planning to pass through and had commissioned them to heal the sick and to proclaim the nearness of God's rule. They were ordinary disciples, these seventy, though they were given exactly the same message as the twelve apostles had been given a short time before. All, whether apostles or ordinary disciples, were sent on the same mission and given the same authority and the same message. Luke 10:17–20 reads:

And the seventy returned with joy, saying, 'Lord, even the devils are subject unto us in thy name'. And he said unto them, 'I beheld Satan fallen as lightning from heaven. Behold, I have given you authority to tread upon serpents and scorpions, and over all the power of the enemy: and nothing shall in any wise hurt you. Howbeit in this rejoice not, that the spirits are subject unto you; but rejoice that your names are written in heaven.'

In this passage we first note the reality of the spiritual world of evil and the reality of the conflict with evil. Indeed, it is the most striking feature of the passage, this spiritual nature of the conflict in which the Christian ministry and, indeed, every Christian is engaged.

The reality of this spiritual world and spiritual conflict is in sharp contrast with the way we ordinarily look at the world today. Jesus, God's Son, took the spiritual world of evil very seriously. He spoke much of Satan, the devil, the prince of this world – 'the enemy', as he calls him in this passage.

The world of spiritual wickedness is a reality. Jesus met it in conflict at the beginning of his ministry in the temptations. Satan is at work in God's world. The woman afflicted with sickness for eighteen years, Jesus told the synagogue leader, was bound by Satan with that sickness. And in Acts 10:38 Peter told Cornelius that Jesus, in his ministry, had gone about doing good and healing the sickness of those who were oppressed by the devil. At the end of his ministry, Jesus told Peter that Satan had wished to have him to sift him like wheat. It was through Jesus' prayers that the devil's machinations and purposes were thwarted, and Peter himself later described the devil as like a roaring lion going about seeking whom he could devour (*1 Pet. 5:8*).

The world of evil is a reality. Jesus saw his death on the cross as victory over the spiritual powers of wickedness. Through it he overcame the world and through it the prince of this world was cast out, as he said in John 12. And the rest of the New Testament testifies to the same truth, that we are engaged in a spiritual conflict with evil in the heavenly places, as Paul says in Ephesians 6. The Book of Revelation makes very clear the reality of this conflict which God is engaged in through Christ and through Christians. We must be aware of this, we must keep our eye fixed on our target. Our attention, our ministry, must not be engrossed with projects, plans and activities of ministry, which have only a slight heavenly dimension and are essentially temporal things belonging to this world.

[67]

Today we have very largely lost sight of the fact that it is Satan and spiritual evil that we are up against. Our interests and our energies are directed at, and our prayers are absorbed by, all sorts of lesser objectives and projects for their own sake. Yet the conflict is a real one. In this passage Jesus calls Satan 'the enemy'. We must not lose sight of the enemy. Field Marshal Montgomery, when he was fighting General Rommel in the Libyan desert, had a photograph of Rommel hanging in his field headquarters caravan because, as he said, he never wanted to forget who the enemy was and what he might be up to. Our world view must never neglect the spiritual world and the spiritual powers of evil which are engaged in fighting God and his purposes and with whom God, through Christ and us, is in conflict.

Firstly, the Luke passage quoted above teaches us that the conflict is real but, secondly, that the victory is also real. The seventy came back from the mission full of joy because they had seen, demonstrated before their eyes, the defeat of Satan. They exclaimed 'the devils are subject to us in your name'. The conflict, a real one, is a victorious one. It is in the name of Jesus that we engage in this spiritual warfare for the souls of men and for the institutions of society: 'the devils are subject to us *in your name*'. In the name of Jesus victory is assured if we engage in our ministry within the context of the character and name of Christ. Victory is assured because we simply follow the victorious Lamb. 'We march in his army', as Revelation 14:4 expresses it. He has already cast out the prince of this world.

It was on the cross that Christ won the victory when he endured the full penalty of sin, the curse which sin evokes. And he bore this curse triumphantly, for at no point in all that experience, in all that testing and temptation, did his faith or his love for God and his people waver. Christ is the victor. Satan did what he could and failed. Christ overcame by bearing the penalty of our sin. Christ is the victor, the cross is the victory and so the cross must be central in our message and ministry.

The ministry of the seventy anticipated that victory of the cross; they shared in it proleptically, as it were, before the event. The cross cast its shadow before. Jesus saw Satan fall from heaven through the ministry which the seventy exercised in his name. Our ministry is also in his name; it, too, shares in the victory of the cross. Through it, too, Satan falls, for Christ shares his triumphant power with us. As we know from his last words in Matthew, all authority in heaven and on earth has been given to him because he is victor and he shares his authority, which his victory on the cross won, with his people. He says, 'I give you authority to tread on snakes and scorpions and over every power of the enemy and nothing shall in any way hurt you'. Here is authority for one hundred per cent victory. The enemy is real, but we have Christ's authority to tread him underfoot.

The authority that Jesus has given us over every power of the enemy is a spiritual authority over spiritual opposition. We are not promised authority or protection against all the physical ills which Satan may be permitted to inflict (*2 Cor. 12:7*). We have seen that sickness is the oppression of the devil (*Acts 10:38*) and the Epistle to the Hebrews says the devil has the power of death (*2:14*); he exercised this power of death not long afterwards against the apostle James and the martyr Stephen. So, plainly, the promise 'nothing shall in any way hurt you', which was only spoken a few years at most before these men's deaths, is not in the physical realm.

It is not authority over the physical inflictions of sickness or death with which Satan distresses us, though these too, of course, are within the wise sovereignty of God's good purposes, but it is authority over every spiritual evil of the enemy which we have been given, and we should exercise our ministry with this assurance from Christ for certain victory, for Christ has graciously joined us with himself in his victory.

Christ has cast out Satan from heaven and he saw the mission of the seventy as part of this. Satan fell from heaven through their ministry. And Christ gives to us the same ministry and the same authority and the same certainty of victory in his name. The conflict is real and we should never forget it. The victory is certain and we should go forward in confidence.

We should turn to the apostles' example to find the way in which we are to engage in this victorious conflict, this spiritual ministry to which Christ sends us. It is by giving ourselves to prayer and to the Word of God. The apostles summarized their ministry in Acts 6:4 as: 'we will continue steadfastly in prayer, and in the ministry of the word'. Prayer is primary. It was through prayer that Jesus defeated Satan's intentions to sift Peter as wheat. 'I have prayed for you,' he told his apostle (*Luke 22:32*). Again, it was through prayer that Jesus cast out the intransigent evil spirit from the epileptic boy for, in answer to his disciples' enquiry, 'Why could not we cast it out?', he replied, 'this kind comes not forth but by prayer' (*Matt. 17:19, 21*). Raising Lazarus, he thanked his heavenly Father that his prayer had been heard.

Prayer is primary in our ministry and yet how little we exercise this powerful battering ram against Satan's strongholds. As we go to our ministry, whether in the ordinary daily avocations of life as lay people or in the more specialized ministries of preacher or pastor, we must follow the example of the apostles who told their fellow disciples that they would give themselves to prayer.

Along with prayer the apostles gave themselves to the ministry of the Word. That Word is the same Word that Jesus entrusted to the seventy and, earlier, to the twelve apostles. It is to proclaim the kingdom of God. Proclaiming the kingdom of God means proclaiming the cross, for Christ's death established the kingdom or rule of God. It was there that Jesus the King was, for it was there that Satan was cast out of heaven by the Victor. We are to preach Jesus,

God's anointed one, Jesus the Christ crucified – he who, on the cross, became a curse for us that, triumphant in it, he might be raised to God's throne. We preach Jesus as King. If we preach this message, God will honour it. Satan will fall. Martin Luther had a phrase, 'Let the Word do it', that is the Word of the cross, the Word about the King. Prayer and preaching were the only ministries which the apostles referred to in summarizing their activities in Acts 6.

Our ministry is now only in the heavenlies, in the spiritual realm, for the conspicuous triumphing over Satan in the physical realm through the curing of sickness or raising the dead is a ministry not permanently entrusted by Christ to his disciples after his resurrection. The epistles, for example, do not focus attention on such ministry. We are sent to engage in the much more significant conflict against spiritual wickedness in the souls of men and women and in the institutions of society which they create. Our weapons are spiritual, namely prayer and the Word about Jesus.

Jesus has promised that this ministry will be rewarded with success, spiritual success. We will tread down snakes and scorpions. Nothing will harm us, and so we must address ourselves, unflaggingly, to this commission with the authority we have received to triumph over every power of the enemy. We are joined with Jesus in his warfare against the evil which holds God's creation in servitude. Our conflict is spiritual and our weapons are supernatural. They are a word about Christ in his supernatural power, not just an earthly word or a moralizing word or a pedagogic word about some passage of Scripture, but a word about Christ the King, the coming Judge, the triumpher over Satan. And our prayer, too, must be spiritual, supernatural – not just earthly meditation or rote prayer, but persistent prayer to our heavenly Father in the name of Jesus the Lord and King. 'Men ought always to pray and not to give up', said our Lord (*Luke 18:1*). It must be true prayer, prayer that reaches to the throne of God and dwells in his presence.

The rejoicing seventy were elated because of the evident signs of authority over evil that was theirs through the name of Jesus, but Jesus drew their attention to a much more significant ground for their joy. Their joy was not to rest in success in ministry, even success over so hateful a foe as the enemy of God. Success in one's ministry may not always be obvious and, if it is obvious, it might even be counterfeit with no heavenly dimension to it. Jesus predicted in Matthew 7 that there would be some who cast out devils in his name who were not even Christians and to whom he would say on the day of judgment, 'I never knew you: depart from me, workers of iniquity' (*vv. 22, 23*). Each of us – whether clergyman or lay person – should examine our consciences to see how we stand with Jesus the Lord.

Is he our Lord? Are we making his ministry of conflict with Satan through prayer and the word of the cross the one object of our serving him? We are, as Peter says, to make our election sure by seeking Christ's face, submitting to him in obedience. For, though the obvious success in ministry is indeed something to thank God for when it is given to us by God – and we know that it will be given if we are faithful because we have been given a victorious ministry – yet success in ministry is not to be the basis of our joy in ministry. Our true joy is to be found in our relationship with our heavenly Father.

'Rejoice not in this,' he told his disciples, 'that the devils are subject to you' – as undoubtedly they were and will also be to us in our ministry – 'but rejoice that your names are enrolled in heaven'. That is, rejoice in the unchanging relationship with God our heavenly Father for he has brought us into his presence through his Spirit. He has adopted us as his sons and his daughters and we speak to him as Father. He has written our names in his book, we are his and he is ours for eternity. That is our real ground for joy and, no matter what the outward circumstances of our life or ministry may be, nothing can affect this joy, for nothing can affect this relationship. And Jesus commands us to rejoice in it. We must ask to what extent we are to be obedient to this command of our Lord, 'rejoice that your names are written in heaven'. How often do we think of being eternally his? How often do we think of it? How often do we thank God for this privilege of being eternally his? How often do we rejoice that he is our inheritance and that we are his portion? For the words of our Lord are plain, 'rejoice in this, that your names are written in heaven'. Let us ask for grace to obey.

Jesus gives us an example of following his own injunction in the next verses where we read, 'In that same hour Jesus rejoiced in spirit and said, "I thank you, Father, because you have revealed these things to babes and sucklings"'. In other words, he gave thanks to his Father that the names of his disciples were written in heaven. We should give thanks continually for one another's faith and for the grace of being his forever. Strengthened with this true joy, we will be enabled to go forth to this ministry of conflict with evil, giving ourselves to prayer and the Word of God, exercising the authority given to us by our Lord over every power of the enemy, in the assurance that nothing shall in any way hurt us.

There is joy in ministry in the name of the Lord, as the seventy realized, for it is a victorious ministry. There is joy in ministry and we should all taste it. But there is greater, more serene joy in the relationship with God on which this ministry is based. So, as we minister in his name, we should be obedient to the command of our Lord and rejoice greatly, rejoice continually, that our names, with the names of our fellow Christians, the fellow members of our congregation, are written by God in heaven.

Appendix

SOME NOTES ON PRINCIPLES FOR CONDUCTING TRAINING FOR THE MINISTRY[1]

1. THE SELECTION of entrants to ensure that all have a true commitment to Christ as Lord, and may have personal gifts which enable them to relate naturally to other people; have intellectual ability, having attained at least university entrance standards; have a call to preach the gospel, that is, are sent by God into his harvest and are not merely altruists motivated to help people in this life – for such will not last the distance and will find themselves shut in to a ministry to which God has not sent them.

2. THE CURRICULUM to ensure that, on the completion of the four-year course, students will have a grasp of the contents of the whole Bible as God's infallible Word and of its teaching, so as to grasp the whole counsel of God; that is, to understand the Bible as a unified whole and to apprehend the concepts of the mind of God revealed in it, so as to come into deeper fellowship with God and to be equipped to bring others into the same knowledge of him.

   Four years' full-time study after obtaining university

[1]These notes were written at Cambridge in 1980 and are, in part, descriptive of the author's vision for the ongoing work of Moore Theological College, Sydney.

entrance is the minimum for basic ministerial education in today's culture.

Biblical languages. On the completion of the four-year course, students should have read at least ten chapters of the Hebrew Bible and one hundred chapters of the Greek New Testament, and have enough fluency in these languages to be able to continue reading them in later ministry, if they chose (as indeed they ought!).

Systematic biblical theology and *Christian* (i.e. biblical) *ethics* are closely related. During the course, students should have read certain designated *Christian classics* (including Calvin's *Institutes*, the most important handbook of Christian theology so far written). A select list of these should be drawn up as required (but unexamined) reading.

Church history. The history of Christians, how they acted, suffered and thought, is an aid to apprehending more clearly the teaching of the Bible and is indispensable in understanding the modern situation in which the Christian faith is to be lived and proclaimed.

The knowledge of *philosophy*, i.e., the various ways in which human existence has been apprehended, is an aid to understanding the situation to which the gospel is addressed and indispensable in proclaiming the gospel in an educated and sophisticated society.

Liturgiology is the history of and an analysis of the biblical principles which should control Christians when they meet in company together to meet with Christ and one another.

Pastoral counselling. This is a subdivision of Christian ethics, for counselling is a duty that all Christians have to each other. Many topics are included, such as comforting the bereaved, bringing up children, how to relate as husband and wife, caring for the indigent (including a knowledge of the local welfare agencies).

Communication technology and praxis. In addition to

apprehending from the Bible the whole counsel of God, including the consequences for Christian relationship to God, man and the world, the curriculum aims to include an introduction to the practical art of conveying the Christian message by ministers of the Word.

This will embrace the principles and practice of:

(a) evangelism;
(b) preaching;
(c) teaching the young;
(d) teaching adults;
(e) leading common worship when meeting together to meet with Christ.

If there is any time left in the course, the future minister may be given introductory instruction in the set-up and methods of ministry customary in the local denomination, e.g., how to conduct a wedding or funeral and how to administer a parish. Otherwise, if time is lacking, this elementary instruction (together with further instruction) may be left to the early years of the ordained minister. If students are not taught the whole counsel of God during their college course, most will not pick it up later as an integrated whole on which to base their ministry. Therefore teaching this has priority, if time is short.

3. FACULTY. The third most important principle is the selection and encouragement of the teaching faculty. The members of the faculty should be spiritually-minded persons devoted to the lordship of Christ, heavenly-oriented, fully committed to the infallibility of Holy Scripture and convinced that a knowledge of God through the Bible is the source of Christian living and ministry. They should also be convinced of the vital importance of ministry within the congregation.

They should have fully-developed personal qualities. They should be intellectually gifted and should have capitalized on these natural gifts by academic attainment, or be in the process of doing so. They should be able to communicate in sermon, classroom and personal relationship.

The quality of the teaching faculty may well be regarded as the primary principle for the conducting of the college. In other words, although the first three principles listed above may be regarded as ranking equally in importance, nevertheless, if a choice has to be made between them, the quality of the teaching faculty undoubtedly ranks first. For a faculty that is first rate in all these areas will draw the right students and the faculty will create and teach the right curriculum.

4. THE LIBRARY. This is the fourth most important principle. A good library will support a good faculty and draw a good, studious student body.

5. SIZE OF STAFF. The teaching faculty should not be less than 12 members, if the whole curriculum is to be covered in depth, nor less than one full-time member (or equivalent) to ten students (or eleven if student numbers are large), if students are to be given proper pastoral and tutorial care, and the faculty are to have time to deepen their own Christian knowledge. The faculty should be distributed in age (i.e. seniority).

6. SPIRITUAL LIFE. The formation of the spiritual life of the faculty and students of the College is an ongoing activity, and should arise naturally from college activities. Prayer and teaching are the instrument. Chapel is held daily; all members of the college are expected to be present. The

liturgy is followed and sermons are preached daily by faculty and final-year students.

The college is divided into groups of 4, 5 or 6 students, spanning the college years, who meet weekly for prayer together. There is also a weekly communal prayer meeting for all.

Since everything in life is related to God, every subject in the curriculum should be related to God. Some subjects will be more clearly related to God in his relationships in himself and to his creation than others but all the lectures should have a teaching element of 'God's whole counsel' and consequently will not only stimulate the mind but also affect the heart, the conscience and the will.

Regular sermons should be preached by the faculty (and final-year students) in the college chapel (at which all attend), expounding God's Word. If it is truly God's Word that the preacher is speaking to the hearer, it will be living and powerful, reaching right down through the mind into the conscience and so form the spiritual life of the college.

Knowledge is the basis of godliness. It was for knowledge that Paul prayed for his converts.

The whole college, i.e. all students and all faculty members, go on evangelistic missions for one week each year, in different churches, staying in the homes of members of the congregation.

All students take part in regular ministry in a congregation on Sundays, as do also junior members of the faculty. Older members may also do so, or accept invitations to preach in different congregations.

The Christian life is knowing Christ, that is, being consciously in the presence of the true Lord. This is faith from which flow thanks, love, trust, obedience, hope.

Three things flow into knowing Christ as a person, as our Lord, our Friend, and our Saviour on the day of judgement:

(a) His speaking to us through his Word preached, read publicly and privately, spoken by pastor or friend. His sheep hear his voice.

(b) Our speaking to him in prayer in line with his character, i.e. prayer in his name, and by meditation on his word (Psa. 1:2). (N.B.: not mere vacuous religious meditation, which is harmful and evil.)

(c) Christian fellowship, that is, sharing with one another the things of Christ.

The theological college should make provision and opportunity for these three things and promote them by instruction, exhortation and, if necessary, admonition. In this way its members will grow in godliness by growing in their personal knowledge and relationship with their Lord and also with one another through the consequential obedience of lovingly serving one another.

SOME OTHER
BANNER OF TRUTH
TITLES

NOT BY BREAD ALONE

God's Word on Present Issues

David Broughton Knox

Man cannot live by bread alone says Jesus. When stated so simply and starkly this truth seems obvious; yet so much of late twentieth-century life underlines how often it is ignored. Society lies in the grip of a mind-set which sees man as the measure of all things. This fundamental lack of perspective affects his whole life and means that he can never see the real answer to his own deepest problems.

In *Not by Bread Alone*, D. Broughton Knox discusses a wide variety of issues in the contemporary world in which this spiritual short-sightedness has had alarming consequences. He shows how it has distorted and impoverished our experience in personal, local, national and international life.

Listening to the word of man alone has produced a devastating famine of the spirit. Broughton Knox guides us to the only reliable nourishment and to the remedy which Jesus himself prescribed: the teaching of Scripture. With skill, insight and wisdom, he applies it to critical areas of twentieth-century life and points us to a style of life that is centred on God, and therefore both satisfying and enriching.

Dr Broughton Knox was for many years Principle of Moore Theological College, Sydney, Australia. Now in official retirement he is actively serving in the newly-founded George Whitefield College in Kalk Bay, South Africa.

ISBN 0 85151 565 7
156pp. Paperback.

THE CHRISTIAN MINISTRY

Charles Bridges

The revival of the Church seems to be closely connected with the condition of its ministry. Bridges sub-titled his study of the Christian ministry, '*An Inquiry into the Causes of its Inefficiency*', and, rightly used, it is well suited to promote a faithful and effective ministry.

Charles Bridges (1794–1869) was one of the leaders of the Evangelical party in the Church of England in the last century. He was vicar of Old Newton, Suffolk, from 1823 to 1849, and later of Weymouth and Hinton Martell in Dorset. *The Christian Ministry* is Bridges' best-known literary work, but his expositions of *Proverbs, Ecclesiastes* and *Psalm 119* are also highly valued.

Bridges begins by considering the general and personal causes of ministerial ineffectiveness, and goes on to examine comprehensively preaching and pastoral work. This book was one of the few which the godly Robert Murray M'Cheyne took with him to the Holy Land, and, in its field, it is without an equal.

ISBN 0 85151 087 6
408pp. Cloth-bound.

FAITH AND LIFE

B. B. Warfield

B. B. Warfield (1851–1921) stands as one of the greatest of Reformed theologians. He taught for over thirty years at Princeton Seminary, achieving an enormous output of learned and massive books and articles in defence of historic Calvinism.

Faith and Life reveals another side of the man. Warfield kept up the Princeton tradition of Sunday afternoon classes with the students of the Seminary in which, in his own words, 'the deeper currents of Christian faith and life' were explored. This book contains some of the memorable addresses he gave on those occasions. Always based on careful use of Scripture (Warfield has been called 'a master of the Scripture's meaning'), they are informal yet restrained, urgent yet tender.

The learned theologian had a child-like confidence in his Saviour and in the reality of his own Christian experience. He once told his students, 'In your case there can be no "either-or", either a student or a man of God. You must be both.' Warfield himself was both, as these pages reveal.

Among the various subjects dealt with, two stand out: the work of the Spirit in conviction, faith, adoption, and prayer; and the need for true devotion to Christ and his cause.

Although, on Warfield's death, Gresham Machen believed that 'old Princeton' had died with him, this book can help the type of piety, long eclipsed, for which Warfield stood, to shine forth in its fulness again.

ISBN 0 85151 585 1
468pp. Cloth-bound.

THE REFORMED PASTOR

Richard Baxter

Richard Baxter (1615–1691) was vicar of Kidderminster from 1647 to 1661. In an Introduction to this reprint, Dr J. I. Packer describes him as 'the most outstanding pastor, evangelist and writer on practical and devotional themes that Puritanism produced'. His ministry transformed the people of Kidderminster from 'an ignorant, rude and revelling people' to a godly, worshipping community. These pages, first prepared for a Worcestershire association of ministers in 1656, deal with the means by which such changes are ever to be accomplished. In his fervent plea for the discharge of the spiritual obligations of the ministry, Baxter, in the words of his contemporary, Thomas Manton, 'came nearer the apostolic writings than any man in the age'. A century later Philip Doddridge wrote, '*The Reformed Pastor* is a most extraordinary book . . . many good men are but shadows of what (by the blessing of God) they might be, if the maxims and measures laid down in that incomparable Treatise were strenuously pursued.' Today, Baxter's principles, drawn from Scripture and re-applied in terms of modern circumstances, will provide both ministers and other Christians with challenge, direction and help.

ISBN 0 85151 191 0
256pp. Paperback.

For free illustrated catalogue please write to
THE BANNER OF TRUTH TRUST
3 Murrayfield Road, Edinburgh EH12 6EL
PO Box 621, Carlisle, Pennsylvania 17013, USA